The U.S. Marines in the
Second Creek and
Second Seminole Wars

Fort Brooke Tampa Bay (picture from the Florida State Archives)

The U.S. Marines in the Second Creek and Second Seminole Wars

By

David Ekardt

Bookbaby Press

Ingramspark

Copyright August 2013

Acknowledgements

I wish to acknowledge the following people for the assistance they gave in the compilation of this work. Their knowledge and expertise was most helpful and inspiring.

Jesse (Archie) Marshall Ranger Veterans Park, Tampa, Florida

Dale Burridge historian

Greg Centane historian

Greg Cena United States Marine Corps Archives

Gary Ellis Archaeologist State of Florida

James Cusick librarian curator University of Florida Library Special Collections

Dedication

For my Marine Brothers of 1st Radio Battalion

Vietnam and Hawaii

Semper Fi!

The Removal Act
28 May 1830

An Act to provide for an exchange of lands with the Indians residing in any of the states or territories, and for their removal west of the river Mississippi.

Be it enacted by the Senate and House of Representatives of the United States of America, in Congress assembled, That it shall and may be lawful for the President of the United States to cause so much of any territory belonging to the United States, west of the river Mississippi, not included in any state or organized territory, and to which the Indian title has been extinguished, as he may judge necessary, to be divided into a suitable number of districts, for the reception of such tribes or nations of Indians as may choose to exchange the lands where they now reside, and remove there; and to cause each of said districts to be so described by natural or artificial marks, as to be easily distinguished from every other.

And be it further enacted, That it shall and may be lawful for the President to exchange any or all of such districts, so to be laid off and described, with any tribe or nation of Indians now residing within the limits of any of the states or territories, and with which the United States have existing treaties, for the whole or any part or portion of the territory claimed and occupied by such tribe or nation, within the bounds of any one or more of the states or territories, where the land claimed and occupied by the Indians, is owned by the United States, or the United States are bound to the state within which it lies to extinguish the Indian claim thereto.

And be it further enacted, That in the making of any such exchange or exchanges, it shall and may be lawful for the President solemnly to assure the tribe or nation with which the exchange is made, that the United States will forever secure and guaranty to them, and their heirs or successors, the country so exchanged with them; and if they prefer it, that the United States will cause a patent or grant to be made and executed to them for the same: Provided always, That such lands shall revert to the United States, if the Indians become extinct, or abandon the same.

And be it further enacted, That if, upon any of the lands now occupied by the Indians, and to be exchanged for, there should be such improvements as add value to the land claimed by any individual or individuals of such tribes or nations, it shall and may be lawful for the President to cause such value to be ascertained by appraisement or otherwise, and to cause such ascertained value to be paid to the person or persons rightfully claiming such improvements. And upon the payment of such valuation, the improvements so valued and paid for, shall pass to the United States, and possession shall not afterwards be permitted to any of the same tribe.

And be it further enacted, That upon the making of any such exchange as is contemplated by this act, it shall and may be lawful for the President to cause such aid and assistance to be furnished to the emigrants as may be necessary and proper to enable them to remove to, and settle in, the country for which they may have exchanged; and also, to give them such aid and assistance as may be necessary for their support and subsistence for the first year after their removal.

And be it further enacted, that it shall and may be lawful for the President to cause such tribe or nation to be protected, at their new residence, against all interruption or disturbance from any other tribe or nation of Indians, or from any other person or persons whatever.

And be it further enacted, That it shall and may be lawful for the President to have the same superintendence and care over any tribe or nation in the country to which they may remove, as contemplated by this act, that he is now authorized to have over them at their present places of residence: Provided, That nothing in this act contained shall be construed as authorizing or directing the violation of any existing treaty between the United States and any of the Indian tribes.

And be it further enacted, that for the purpose of giving effect to the Provisions of this act, the sum of five hundred thousand dollars is hereby appropriated, to be paid out of any money in the treasury, not otherwise appropriated.

Contents

Author's replica Marine Gear

Preface

When I started out to write an article about the Marine involvement in the Second Seminole War I found there was so little written about them in any one source and no one had ever made a complete compilation of this topic. Even in the Marine history books, not more than a few paragraphs were devoted to the topic. What started out as an article evolved into a book as I uncovered several sources of information, a few lines here, a paragraph there in many different types of works. Unfortunately though much of the documentation of Commandant Colonel Henderson written during the war period was lost in a wagon fire.

Although this was going to be a work on the Second Seminole War, the Marine involvement in the Second Creek War that started about the same time could not be excluded from the work. Both flared up at the same time, and Henderson and the Marine regiment first assisted in the Creek conflict in Georgia and Alabama, and on to Florida to join the fray with the Seminoles. In researching both conflicts, It came as a total surprise to learn first from the Army Navy Chronicles of the time, then from other sources that Marines and Marine officers were actually in charge of groups of Indians in their removal to the Arkansas Territory that later became Oklahoma. A few of the officers were assigned to lead the groups of Creek Indians from Alabama to the west, then later Seminoles from Florida.

Both conflicts were a result of the Indian Removal Act. President Andrew Jackson managed to get his Indian Removal Act through Congress in 1830, which ordered the removal of all Indians from east of the Mississippi River to the Arkansas Territory. This included not only the bands of Indians but of the 'civilized' Indians (mostly Choctaw and Cherokee) who had settled into the white man's ways, establishing farms, schools churches and communities.

Part of the problem with the Seminole situation in Florida, was the fact that many run away slaves were living amongst the Seminoles as free men and as slaves. There was much friction along the Georgia-

Florida border as slave catchers ran back and forth across the border retaking those escaped slaves as they

could. This led to reprisals from the Seminoles who would attack plantations and settlements in north

Florida and southern Georgia. This culminated in the start of the Seminole War when Major Francis

Dade's command of over one hundred men were attacked on the military road between Fort Brooke

(Tampa) and Fort King (Ocala) were massacred in December 1835.

The Creek War broke out at the same time after groups of Creeks who did not want

to comply with the removal act, attacked plantations in Alabama and Georgia. The local

governments called on the federal government for assistance.

President Jackson, who earlier had tried to abolish the Marine Corps soon realized

he could not manage both of these situations without the assistance of the Marines and

the militias of several states.

In May 1836, Colonel Commandant Archibald Henderson offered the services of his

Marines. In General Jesup's 1836 Diary of the Creek Campaign, his entry of May 21, 1836 reads:

"Offered Major General Gardner the appointment of Inspector General. Colonel Henderson volunteered

his corps which was accepted by the Secretary of War, ad sanctioned by the President". According to

Marine legend, Henderson then sent word out to the contingents at the naval yards to pack their gear and

prepare to move south. He is alleged to have tacked a note to his office door at Marine Headquarters in

Washington that read, *"Gone to Fight Indians, be back when the war is over. A. Henderson"*.

His men were quick to move and join the fray. It was the largest mobilization of the

Corps since the war of 1812, and the first time Marines moved to war on a train. Fleet

Marines of the West Indies Squadron had already started to reinforce the Army troops in

Florida, so Henderson's regiment was sent to Georgia and Alabama to assist the state

militias and army under General Thomas Sidney Jessup. They were there from May until

October 1836 when their job there was done, they were sent to Florida with Jesup.

The Second Seminole War was a war of innovations. India rubber boats were used,

as well as wagons with extra wide 'tires' to deal with the sandy roads, and also lined with

India rubber to keep cargo dry in the many stream crossings. Steamboats were put to

use in this conflict also for the first time. The Hall breach loading rifle was introduced with

many troops as well as Colt's repeating rifle, which did not perform well. Sam Colt also toured Florida

with his new revolvers demonstrating them to the officers and sold them to anyone who wanted them.

Riverine warfare was also introduced in the Everglades and many rivers in Florida.

The Marines proved to be versatile and adaptable to the many varied tasks given to

them. They built and manned forts, they made amphibious landings, they patrolled rivers

and the Everglades in specially made canoes, they led volunteer Creek Indian troops,

and they formed a mounted Marine force that General Jessup used as a quick

reactionary force, both Henderson and finally Lt. Colonel Samuel Miller were put in charge of Fort

Brooke at Tampa Bay, to include managing the port, the moving of supplies, overseeing other troops

stationed there. Finally, they also over saw the removal and transportation of the many groups of Indians

to the western lands that were to become their new home.

I have inserted many direct references from the participants as it is always best to learn history from those who lived it and made it and not 'revised' by the author.

These events of our history have been somewhat glossed over and ignored. This was a period of 'nation building' as espoused by President Andrew Jackson as *"extending the area of freedom"*, later known as 'Manifest Destiny', to have our nation stretch from the Atlantic to the Pacific. The several tribes of Indians posed a problem in the

effort to achieve that. There were many conflicts when the two cultures clashed. There

was enough blame for those problems on both sides of the argument. The solution that

was decided upon was to move the Indians to an area out of the way to end the

conflicts. To separate the two was to have peace as was the prevailing thought.

To some of that period, it was the right solution for many had lost family and friends to the constant fighting. To others it seemed atrocious to take people from their homes and

force them to move. Many saw the Indians struggling to hold on to their homes as

noble. To others not. Greed for the fertile lands that the original occupants had led to

many of the problems. In the middle of this was thrown the military to enforce the law of

the land.

The Marines did their duty no matter how they felt about it and some of that shows in

the letters that survived. This work was not written to endorse nor condemn what transpired, only to make a comprehensive compilation of what the Marines did during these years of conflict. Although this is the most complete work on their involvement, it is still incomplete. The actions of the Marines of the West Indies Squadron and the 'Mosquito Fleet' are well documented as well as much of what Lt. Col. Samuel Miller's actions were thanks to the journals of General Jesup. Also, the involvement of the officers who were charged with taking the Creeks and Seminoles out west. However what Colonel Henderson and his command in Alabama and Florida did is still not well documented due to the loss of his reports and letters.

As noted in the Bibliography many of the sources listed are journals and letters from some of the Navy and Army participants, some of which came to light many years later as they were found in family collections and brought to light. Perhaps one day more such journals and letters may turn up to shed light on what these Marines did during the conflicts.

The Seminole war proved to be the longest and most expensive of the Indian wars. During this war, there were four different commanders. Major General Winfield Scott commanded between March and April 1836. He failed in his attempt to bring the Seminoles into a fixed large scale battle. He had very little knowledge of the terrain and his opponents. He was replaced by the new Florida governor Richard Keith Call, whom President Jackson was familiar with. He commanded from June to December 1836. He too failed in his attempts to bring the Seminoles to a major battle.

Major General Sidney Jesup then came to Florida and took over between December 1836 and May 1838. He had the most success of all. He utilized all the resources that he could. These included regular troops, militia from other states, the Navy, Marines and Creek warriors. He was adaptable in his methods. When his attempts to use the same tactics as his predecessors failed, he switched to using the Mounted Marines and other cavalry forces as quick reactionary forces. Jesup employed hammer and anvil operations, and sweeps of areas, keeping the Seminoles on the move. His troops destroyed abandoned villages, crops, confiscated cattle and anything that the Seminoles needed for subsistence.

He also used negotiations and eventually captured several chiefs including Osceola by luring them in under flags of truce, then taking them prisoner. For this the public condemned him. He also came under fire when the Indians who surrendered in large numbers in 1837, suddenly disappeared from their encampment near Fort Brooke and returned to fighting. In negotiations, he went against official policy by allowing the Seminoles to take their Negro slaves and tribal members with them to the west rather than surrender them to be returned to slavery or in many cases of those who were born free, to be condemned to a life of slavery. In all, Jesup managed to obtain the surrender of almost 3,000 Seminoles and had them transported to new lands in the west.

Jesup was replaced by Brigadier Zachery Taylor from May 1838 to April 1840; Taylor introduced a new strategy of dividing Florida into districts with a fort built in the middle of each with units constantly patrolling their district. He built roads and bridges throughout the territory facilitating the movement of troops and supplies. He too did his best to negotiate with the Indians. This led to a cease fire with the promise of the remaining Indians to stay in Florida. This did not last. He was also condemned by the public when news of his importing blood hounds from Cuba to track down the Indians. As it turned out, the use of the dogs did not work and was stopped.

Brigadier General Walker Armistead came next from May 1840 to May 1841. He followed Taylor's strategy of keeping units on the move in their districts and searching out the fields planted by the Seminoles and destroying them. He was replaced by Colonel William Worth from June 1841 to September 1842. He too kept up the pressure on the Seminoles now pushed into the south of Florida below Lake Okeechobee and the Everglades. He made effective use of Navy Lt. McLaughlin's sailors and Marines of the Mosquito Fleet of canoes and small boats. They made inroads all through the Everglades, keeping the remaining small bands constantly on the move and destroying their crops. Whenever his men captured Indians, they were enticed to lead them to their bands in hiding.

Colonel Worth, who by then was in charge of the war effort finally convinced the War Department that there was fewer than 500 Seminoles left, and got permission to negotiate an end of hostilities and leave them in the Everglades. Thus ended the longest of the Indian wars.

Chapter 1

Prelude to War

Marines-Indian Fighters?

Wood engraving from 1836 pamphlet by Captain James Barr (Florida State Archives)

Several things led up to the Creek and Seminole Wars. The trouble started brewing with agreements between the parties, both sides of whom did not do well in living up to their parts of the bargains.

The first treaty between Creek Indians at the end of the First Creek Indian War signed at Fort Jackson in August 1814 forced the Creeks to surrender 2 million acres of land. Over one thousand Red Stick Creeks refused to comply and fled to Florida.

The Moultrie Creek Treaty of September 1823, resulted in the Florida Indians being given over five million acres south of the Peace River, after relinquishing over twenty four million acres.

The Payne's Landing Treaty of May 1832, in line with the Indian Removal Act negotiated between James Gadsden and fifteen Seminole chiefs encouraged the tribes to relocate to the Arkansas territory (later known as Oklahoma).

The Indians insisted on sending a delegation to inspect the new lands. Some believed the Army bribed a translator to mislead the chiefs.

The Fort Gibson Treaty of May1833 signed by the seven Seminole delegates who went to inspect the land in Arkansas, signed under duress .This treaty was the basis for the Indians wanting to go to war.

President Andrew Jackson, no friend to the Indian, had managed to get his 'Indian Removal Act' passed through Congress. It was not a sure deal with many in Congress fighting against it, most notable, Congressman Davy Crockett, who had fought Indians with Jackson during the Creek Indian war of 1818.

The new legislation opened the way to remove all Indians east of the Mississippi River, and locate them out West. This affected many Cherokee, Creek, Choctaw and other Indians who had become 'civilized' adapting to white man ways. These were scattered throughout the south, in Georgia, Alabama, Tennessee and the Carolinas. Many had established farms, schools, businesses, churches and communities. They had adapted to white man's clothing and life styles. This legislation also included removing all the Seminole Indians from Florida.

This war also became one for reclaiming runaway slaves from Florida. Many slaves from northern Florida and Georgia had escaped to the interior of Florida, either willingly, or as captives of the Seminoles.

These former slaves as Seminole slaves lived more freely in the Seminole settlements, having free reign of the settlement, and many owning their own cattle and crops. Others who were not slaves, blended into the settlements, intermarrying, and some even becoming leaders of their tribes.

There had been some fighting along the Florida-Georgia border prior to the war as slave hunters and owners raided Seminole settlements trying to reclaim their 'property'. In return, Seminoles would raid isolated plantations.

The fact that so many slaves had escaped to Florida and the knowledge of this spreading throughout the south, prompted slave owners to put pressure on the government to take action. Many feared the knowledge of freedom in Florida would lead to a slave revolt. These combined events are what led up to what became the longest and most expensive of the Indian Wars of this nation-the Second Seminole War.

Incidents leading up to the Creek War started January 26th 1836, Georgia Militia attack a Creek Indian camp on the Chattahoochee River, in Stewart County Georgia. During a second round of fighting, the militia was driven off. May 5th Jim Henry and Neamathla, Creek leaders, attacked settlers along the Chattahoochee River between Columbus, Georgia and Tuskegee, Alabama with their followers. A week later they attacked a stagecoach outside Fort Mitchell, Alabama. A few days later, Jim Henry, a Hitachi Creek and his warriors attacked and destroyed the town of Roanoke, Georgia, driving the survivors into Columbus, Georgia. Several more attacks on stagecoaches result in the stopping all traffic on the federal road between Montgomery, Alabama, and Columbus.

Incidents leading up to the war in Florida. Early December 1835, Seminoles and Florida militia clashed near Waachoota, and a wood cutting party on Drayton's Island on the St John's River was attacked by

Seminoles. On the 17th of December, Seminoles attacked plantations at Micanopy. The next day they attacked a militia supply train near Waachoota between Newmansville and Micanopy. Two days later, the militia attacked the Seminole's camp and retrieved their wagons, but all the ammunition was gone. The 25th-27th of December, King Philip, his son Caocoochee along with Creek and Yuchie Indians attacked and destroyed all the plantations on the East Coast, capturing many slaves, and driving settlers into St. Augustine for protection. Also during that time, they destroyed a plantation at present day new Smyrna and the Hillsboro lighthouse at present day Fort Lauderdale.

Then Osceola's murder of Indian Agent Wiley Thompson and companion at Fort King Florida, along with the attack on Dade's column so shocked and enraged the nation and ensured that war would follow. The newspapers of the nation fanned the flames which finally moved the nation into war on both fronts.

Chapter 2

MAJOR PARTICIPANTS OF THE WARS

The Presidents:

Andrew Jackson in office 1829–1837 managed to pay off the federal debt. He got his Indian Removal Act passed through Congress and during his time in office over 45,000 Indians were relocated to the Arkansas Territory.

Martin Van Buren in office 1837-1841 continued Jackson's policies keeping the relocation of the Indians as a priority.

William Henry Harrison in office 1841 for only 32 days died of pneumonia.

John Tyler in office 1841-1845 a believer in a strong military, he increased the number of ships in the Navy and brought an end to the Second Seminole War.

The Military Leaders

Major Francis Dade of the 4th U.S. Infantry, led a column of 108 troops from Fort Brooke to Fort King on December 23rd, 1835. They were attacked on December 28th by Seminoles with only 3 survivors, only two of whom made it back to Fort Brooke. This 'massacre' spurred the nation into the longest and most expensive Indian war in its history.

General Edmund Gaines took charge in Florida, his men were the first to reach the site of the Dade Massacre, and buried the dead. His command was later pinned down by Seminoles at Camp Izard on the Withlacoochee River, until relief arrived led by General Clinch.

General Duncan Clinch fought in the War of 1812, the First Seminole War, and also in the Second Seminole War, until he resigned in April 1836. He had 700 men in his command when he rescued Gaines.

General Scott nicknamed "Old Fuss and Feathers", was the longest serving general in the Army. He briefly took charge of the Army in Florida until he was reassigned by the President.

Governor Richard K. Call President Jackson appointed him as territorial governor of Florida on March 16, 1836. He took charge of the militia and won a couple of engagements against the Seminoles.

General Thomas Sidney Jesup

Picture from the Florida State Archives

General Thomas Sidney Jesup was still Army Quartermaster General when President Jackson put him in charge of the Creek War in Alabama and Georgia, then in Florida fighting the Seminoles. He was the most successful General in capturing and removing the Seminoles. He had the Marines with him in Alabama and Florida. His tactic of capturing Osceola and other Indian chiefs under a flag of truce caused a great deal of controversy. He left Florida in 1838.

Colonel Zachery Taylor nickname "Old Rough and Ready", took over after Jesup was reassigned, and was successful in the Battle of Okeechobee against the Seminoles on 25th of December 1837. He was breveted brigadier-general for his actions. He took charge of the Army in Florida until May 1840.

Brigadier-General Walker Keith Armistead took over after Taylor and kept his men in the field even during the summer months which was unusual as summer was considered the 'sickly season'. He was replaced in May 1841.

Colonel William Jenkins Worth followed Armistead and kept up the pressure on the remaining Seminoles. Congress and the nation tired of war, agreed with Worth when he declared an end to the war on August 14th, 1842. There were less than 500 Seminoles remaining in Florida by then.

General Joseph Marion Hernandez Florida Militia gained infamy when he invited several Seminole chiefs to a conference under a flag of truce, then took them prisoner. He marched the chiefs and escorts through the town of St. Augustine for all to see as they imprisoned them at the fort. Chiefs Osceola, Coa Hadjo, Caocoochee, John Cavallo along with seventy-one warriors, six women, four blacks and their weapons.

The Marines

Colonel Archibald Henderson

Picture from the U.S. Marines Archives

Colonel Archibald Henderson Commandant of the Marine Corps, led his men through the Creek Campaign in Alabama, and the Seminole Campaign in Florida until it appeared that the Seminoles were defeated. He had Creek Indian Volunteers and Alabama Militia troops under his command.

Lt. Colonel Samuel Miller hero of the War of 1812 commanding the Marines at Bladensburg, the last troops to stand in the way of the British troops attempting to enter the capital city Washington. Miller was given the responsibility to oversee Fort Brooke, and the troops and harbor at Tampa Bay, then later the area south of Tampa.

Brevet Lt. Col. William Freeman third in command had commanded the Marines at the Boston Navy Yard.

Major William Dulaney took charge of the Marines after Lt. Col. Miller returned north. Dulaney led his men north after the remainder of the regiment of Marines were released from duty in Florida by General Jesup, leaving only the Marines of the West Indies Squadron in Florida.

Captain John Harris

Picture from the U.S. Marines Archives

Captain John Harris led the mounted Marines. He led the charge at the Hatchee Lustee Creek engagement. He was breveted to major and given the honor of taking reports of the incident to the president. In later years, he became the Commandant upon the death of Henderson.

Lt. John Reynolds was put in charge of groups of Creeks and later Seminoles as they were sent west. In later years, he led the Marine battalion at the Battle of Bull Run during the Civil War.

Lt. John Sprague also was in charge of Creeks whom he led west. In 1837 he resigned from the Marines and joined the Army at the suggestion of his father-in-law. In later years he wrote a history of the Second Seminole War, '*The Origin, Progress and Conclusion of the Seminole War*'.

Lt. Andrew Ross as captain of Creek volunteers, led an attack in the battle at the Cove of the Withlacoochee River and died of wounds received on December 11, 1836. He was the first Marine officer to be killed in action since the war of 1812.

Lt. Thomas Sloan accompanied Lt. Reynolds leading Indians west, and was also very active with his Marines in the Mosquito Fleet patrolling the Everglades later in the war.

The Navy

Commodore Alexander James Dallas Served in the war of 1812, established the Pensacola Naval Yard in 1832, commanding it as well as the West Indies Squadron. He was instrumental in directing the naval actions during the Second Seminole War. The Squadron was spread thin as it had the responsibility of combating piracy in the Gulf of Mexico and the Caribbean, as well as patrolling the waters off the coast of Mexico during the Texas Rebellion at the time of the Seminole War.

Lt. Levin Powell during the early years of the war led small naval patrols along the southern coastal waters and inlets of Florida. He inspired the small boat actions that were perfected by McLaughlin who took over from him in 1839.

Lt. John T. McLaughlin perfected 'Riverine Warfare' through the use of small schooners, gun barges, and specially constructed five-man and ten-man canoes. His command of ninety sailors and sixty Marines were the first non-natives to cross the Everglades from the east coast to the west coast in December 1840-January 1841.

Lt. Leib was put in charge of the schooner *Motto* to protect the citizens in the Keys. Later when he returned to the *Concord*, he was sent ashore with a detachment of sailors and Marines to man Fort Foster in January 1837 for a few months. They staved off a few attacks by Seminoles.

The Adversaries

The Creeks

Opothleyahola an influential speaker in 1836, led 1,500 of his warriors against the rebellious Lower Creek. In 1837, Opothleyahola led 8,000 of his people from Alabama to the Arkansas Territory.

Eneah Emathla In 1836, at eighty years old, led his warriors to retaliate for raids on his people. Later when he and his people emigrated west, he died along the way.

Eneah Micco opponent of Creek removal, fighting the encroachment by land speculators, forced his hand and his leadership in the hostilities of 1836 led directly to the government's orders for the forced removal of all the Creek from Alabama.

Jim Henry led Creeks on an attack against the town of Roanoke, Georgia on the Chattahoochee River and attacked two steamboats on the river.

Jim Boy known as Tustennuggee Emathla raised a band of seven hundred and seventy-six warriors to assist in the fight against the Seminoles. He had been a farmer and he had a wife and 9 children

The Seminoles

Some of the Seminole Chief names had their title attached.

Micco stood for chief or peace leader

Tustenugee meant war leader

Micanopy was the overall chief

Emathla meant leader of a band proven in war

Heneka for second in command

Hadjo for reckless courage

Fixico for fearless conduct

Hills haya for medicine man

Osceola

Picture from the Florida State Archives

Osceola also known as Powell, had migrated from his home in Creek country of Alabama with his

mother after the defeat of the Creeks by General Jackson. His name meant 'Black Drink Singer'. He was

bold and intelligent which gave him rise among the Seminoles. At the Treaty of Payne's Landing, while

other chiefs signed the treaty, Osceola walked up to the table, plunged his knife into the treaty paper,

exclaiming, "This is the only treaty that I make with the whites!" He murdered Chief Charley Emathla

scattering the coins that he had after selling his cattle prior to emigration as a warning to other Seminoles

not to emigrate. He also killed Agent Wiley Thompson and companion at Fort King in December 1835

prior to the attack on Major Dade's command.

Micanopy considered to be the overall chief of the Seminoles prior to the war owned a vast cattle herd and hired as many as a hundred runaway slaves to work for him. After trying to work out a peace deal, he joined the fight until it became apparent that the war was futile. After his capture he was sent west with two hundred other Seminoles.

Charley Emathla one of the influential chiefs. He agreed to the emigration west, however because of this he was killed by Osceola.

Alligator also known as Halpatter-Tustenuggee was one of the chiefs who attacked Dade's Command, also the battle of the Withlacoochee, the siege of Camp Izard, and the battle of Lake Okeechobee. He surrendered not long after the Battle of Lake Okeechobee and sent west. In 1841 he was brought back to Florida to assist in negotiations with remaining Seminoles and was successful in convincing several to give up the fight.

Jumper known as Hemha Micco one of the influential chiefs was captured and sent west. In later years, he became a confirmed Baptist minister and leader of his community.

Cooper known as Osuche, relative of both Micanopy and Osceola, he and his son were killed by troops near Lake Apopka.

Coa Hadjo was one of the party of Seminole chiefs who went West in 1832 to look at the land in the Arkansas Territory for possible settlement for his people. He was influential among his people when they decided on war and was one of the chiefs captured under a flag of truce by General Hernandez at General Jesup's orders.

COACOOCHEE
From an old print

Caocoochee

Picture from the Florida State Archives

Caocoochee known as Wild Cat son of King Philip was one of the most militant and very eloquent. In February 1841, Caocoochee showed up at Tampa dressed in a Shakespearean costume from a wagon full of costumes that they captured from a traveling show troupe.

Sam Jones also known as Abiaka along with Osceola and two hundred followers in 1837, entered the relocation camp at Tampa Bay and convinced them to escape and rejoin the fight. He along with Alligator and Caocoochee led about 400 Seminoles at the battle of Lake Okeechobee against Colonel Zachery Taylor.

Tuskegee and Halleck successfully fought off a naval force led by Lt. Powell at the Loxahatchee River on January 15, 1838. They in turn were attacked by General Jesup and a larger force on the 24th of January, 1838.

Halleck Hadjo and Tuskegee tired of fighting met with General Jesup in 1838 with the proposal that they would stop fighting if they could stay in Florida south of Lake Okeechobee. Jesup relayed the proposal to Washington, however the request was denied.

Chitto Tustenugee also known as Snake Warrior a Miccosukee, leader in south Florida, his island village was raided by troops in 1841, forcing his band of followers into the Everglades. His island is now a preserve in Miramar, Florida.

Halleck Tustenugee also of the Miccosukee's, was said to have slit his sister's throat when she advocated surrender and emigration. Severely wounded in a skirmish around Fort King, his band fought in northern Florida until defeated on April 19, 1842 the last true battle of the war. Many years later, he fought for the Union in the Civil War.

Chakaikee leader of the band of Seminoles who ambushed Colonel Harney's troops at the Caloosahatchee River in 1839, and the leader of the amphibious attack on Indian Key. He was killed by Harney's troops in a raid in December 1840.

Black Seminoles

Abraham

Picture from the Florida State Archives

Abraham born around 1790, originally a slave in Pensacola to a doctor may have been his domestic slave as his bearing spoke of this, he gained influence as an interpreter and counselor. He was probably set free when the British occupied Florida. He was one of two black interpreters at the Treaty of Payne's Landing meetings in 1832

Luis Pacheco also started as a slave born around 1798 and was hired out to be an interpreter between the Seminoles and military as he could read and write, and spoke English, Spanish, French and Seminole. He was hired out to guide Major Dade's command for their march from Fort Brooke to Fort King. He ran to the Indians when they attacked the column, or was captured by them. He may have known of the plan to ambush the troops. Both possibilities are still debated although in later years in Oklahoma, he had always insisted that he had been captured.

King Phillip a chief along the Saint Johns River led many raids on the sugar plantations prior to the official outbreak of the war.

John Caesar also a chief in the Saint Johns River area and joined in the deadly raids in the area. He was killed by Florida local troops after his band made a raid to steal horses two miles from St. Augustine.

John Caballo (also spelled Cavallo) translated to John Horse, was at one point a Seminole slave of Indian, Spanish and African descent. He took his Spanish name from his original owner. As a sub chief he advised Osceola and served as an interpreter. He surrendered in 1838 and was sent to the Arkansas Territory with other Seminoles. He returned in 1839 as an interpreter for the Army to try and convince others to turn themselves in.

Chapter 3

The Creek War

"Have gone to fight the Indians. Be back when the war is over. A. Henderson".

The story of the Marine involvement in the Second Seminole War would not be complete without their involvement in the Creek War of 1836. When fighting broke out in Florida, Creeks in Georgia and Alabama also arose to fight removal.

As soon as the war broke out in Florida, Marines of the West India Squadron were the first to arrive on the scene. When Colonel Commandant Archibald Henderson volunteered a Marine Regiment to fight Indians in Florida, they first fought Creeks in Georgia and Alabama between May 1836 and September 1836 on their way there. During this period, General Jesup had army and Marine officers assigned to the task of leading bands of Indians out west as they surrendered, or were captured.

Four of these Marine officers, Lt. John T. Sprague, Lt. John Harris (later to become Commandant), Lt. Thomas T. Sloan, and Lt. John. G Reynolds (who led the Marine Battalion in the First Battle of Bull Run during the Civil War) made the trips, all of whom were affected by the suffering of their charges. Sprague who later resigned his commission and accepted a commission and good posting as an Army officer, through the insistence of his father-in-law, later penned the book, *'The Origins, Progress and Conclusion of the Florida War'*. His letters about his experience in taking a large group of Indians to Fort Gibson, Arkansas are printed in the book, *'Indian Removal'* by Grant Foreman. He describes in great detail the arduous journey, privations, bad weather and contrary government contractor company, *'The Alabama Emigration Company'*, paid to supply wagons, teamsters and supplies for the Indians. These contractors shorted food, clothing, wagons and other supplies in an effort to make a profit.

What became known as the Second Creek War came about as a result of problems between the groups of Creek Indians and unscrupulous white men. As the Creeks were being prepared to emigrate west, they were allowed to sell their lands, livestock and other belongings that they could not take along. Many found themselves being swindled out of their land, and lawsuits tying up the sales of their lands.

Their main chief, Opothleyahola was arrested on a writ of debt that appears to have been a trumped up charge. He encouraged his people to refuse to emigrate until he was released. On March 11, 1836, Secretary of War Cass ordered Indian commissioners to hasten the investigation of the frauds committed against the Creeks. This would enable the Indians to sell their lands quicker and speed up the emigration.

As this progressed, hostilities broke out. War parties of Hitchiti, Yuchi and Chiahas started attacking whites along the Chattahoochee River. They attacked and burned a stage along the road between Tuskegee, Alabama and Columbus, Georgia, killing some of the occupants. They even attacked and captured two steamboats on the Chattahoochee River near Columbus.

The city of Columbus started filling with people fleeing the attacks, many of whom were responsible for the uprising. Many of the Indians who were not involved in the attacks fled to Fort Mitchell for protection from the whites and for food. As these events unfolded, reports of all the turmoil spurred the government in Washington to act. Secretary Cass ordered Army General Thomas S. Jesup to take troops to Alabama to put down the Creeks and move them west.

Jesup himself had no doubts about what caused the uprising as he wrote to the Governor of Alabama, Governor Clay, *" I have no doubt the war was brought about by interested white men and by half-breeds and by Indians who were their dupes. "* 1 Unlike Governor Schley of Georgia, Clay fully agreed with Jessup and aided in the official investigation of the perpetrators. Schley's only interest was to move the Indians away from Georgia and his borders. Too many people were waiting to make a small fortune in taking over the lands that the Indians had to sell and give up. Many of them also were supplying whiskey to the tribes to further fan the flames.

Chief Opothleyahola was persuaded to enlist some of his warriors in the attempt to put down the hostile elements. He raised a force of three hundred and was able to kill one of the leaders and capture several others. He also managed to raise a larger force bringing the total warriors under him to 1,150 to serve under Jessup.

Three separate groups of hostiles were operating in the area led by Eneah Emathla who was blamed for the uprising, Eneah Micco, and Jim Henry. In Early June a band of friendlies led by Jim Boy, captured Eneah Emathla and turned him in to the army at Fort Mitchell. Shortly after that, around a thousand of his followers turned themselves in.

"Have gone to fight the Indians. Be back when the war is over. A. Henderson".

Marine Corps legend has it that Colonel Commandant Archibald Henderson tacked this note on his office door before leading his Marines to the Indian War.

Henderson offered a Marine regiment to President Jackson after discussion with Army General Jesup. President Jackson had never been fond of the Navy or Marines readily accepted the offer. On May 21,

1836 Henderson ordered all available Marines to link up and head south to join with the Army to fight the Indians. The Marines being under Navy laws and regulations could also be placed under the laws and regulations of the Army when serving with them as per the Act of June 30th 1834 which delineated just whose regulations took precedence in joint operations.

Henderson sent word to the Marine detachments at the naval yards along the eastern seaboard to leave only enough men to constitute a small guard detail at each. The majority of the Marines at each post were to pack their gear and prepare to head south. He left the following members at Marine Headquarters Washington DC and the Washington Naval Yard in the following orders to Lt. Col. R. D. Wainwright::

Headquarters or the Marine Corps

Washington, 1st June, 1836.

Sir:

During my absence on the Campaign against the Creek Indians, I leave you in command at Head Quarters. There will be little other than bureau duty to attend to, with which you are so familiar as to render it unnecessary to give any detailed instructions.

Three Sgts. (for duty) 1 Corpl. & 12 privates are left to furnish a guard for the Navy Yard, to consist of 1 Sgt. 1 Corpl. & 6 privates. One of the Music left behind will have to act lance Corporal as a relief for the guard at the Navy Yard. The Sgt. Major will sleep in barracks. Cpl. Brown has always been detailed to attend to the grounds and outside porches around the house occupied by me; I have to request that he be so continued unless it should be necessary to give him other employment or duty.

Sergt. Triquet is left to assist in attending to the duties at head Quarters. He is a respectable old man, and has no other failing than that which but too often attends an old soldier; he has however almost corrected that behavior.

I leave you a most valuable Soldier in the Sergt. Major whose health entirely incapacitates him from going on the expedition. He is anxious to go but as a matter of duty I have ordered him to remain, as I cannot take any other than able bodied med on such an arduous service.

Since writing the above I have decided to leave the Band, and you will be pleased to divide it into two guards to keep up one Sentinel at Head Quarters. The Drum and Fife Majors, will take alternate days with the Sergt. Major to remain in Barracks in charge of them, so that one of those non-commissioned will be at all times within them.

My clerk Wm. Fulmer, can take charge of the school in Barracks, until the regular teacher returns, and can at the same time attend to the business of this office.

Lt Col R.D.Wainwright	*I am respectfully,*
U.S.Marine Corps,	*Your obedt. Sevt.*
Headquarters,	*Signed, Arch Henderson*
	Col.Commdt. 2

The movement of the Marines were well documented as evidenced by these newspaper articles posted in the Army Navy Chronicles of the time:

PORTSMOUTH, (N. H.) May 28

"The U. S. Marines, from Portsmouth, Charlestown and Brooklyn Navy Yards, consisting of 150 men, sailed yesterday on board the packet ship H. Allen, for Charleston, S. C. under the command of Brevet Lieutenant Colonel Freeman, On their arrival there, they will be joined by the marines from the other navy yards, when the whole force will be under the command of Col. Henderson, the commandant of the corps. Their destination is Fort Mitchell, to co-operate with the army against the

Creek nation. The following is .1 list of the officers :— 1st Company—Capt. English, commanding; Brevet Capt. Macomber; 1st Lieut. Edson, Acting Assistant Q. M; 1st Lt. Watkins; 2d Lt. Baker; 2d Lt. Sloan ; -2d Lt. Caldwell.

2d Company—Capt. Walker, commanding; Brevet Capt. Brevoort; 1st Lieut. Reynolds, Acting Adj't ; 2ᵈ lt Lang; 2d lt McLean; 2lt Whitney; 2d Jo McArdle.—N. Y. Star.

Passengers in the Steam packet Win. Gibbons, for Charleston, Lieut. Col. A. S. Brooks, 4th Artillery—

Major Felix Ansart, 3d Artillery—Major W. L. McClintock, 3d Artillery—Lt. S. H. Drum, 4th Artillery

Lieut. Wm. H. Wall, 3rd Artillery—Asst Surg P. Minis, U. S. Army, with two companies of the 3d

Regiment, U. S. Artillery.—N. Y. Star."

"DOMESTIC INTELLIGENCE.

MOVEMENTS OF TROOPS TO ALABAMA.

The four companies of Artillery ordered to the South from Fort Monroe, embarked at that post on Thursday last in the steam packet South Carolina, for Charleston, 200 in number. The only force now remaining at Fort Monroe, is Major Gardner's company, A.

We learn that the marines from Washington and those at Gosport; will proceed to Charleston in the steam packet Columbus, as soon as possible after their arrival here from Charleston, which will probably be on Sunday morning. Those from Washington are expected here on Saturday morning in the steam boat Columbia. —Norfolk Herald.

Among the passengers in the Steam Boat Kentucky, Capt. Sutton, from Baltimore, arrived yesterday morning, where Gen. Fenwick, of the U. S. Army, Capt. Thompson, his aid, and Lieuts. Waite, and Chambers, on their way to the South. "

"We learn that our respected townsman, Major Smith, Paymaster U. S. Army, will leave with the troops for Charleston.—Norfolk Beacon, May 27. "

"The Philadelphia National Gazette says, "We learn that the marines from all the naval stations, are ordered to the south, to be employed against the Creek Indians if necessary, and to aid in the suppression of the war in Florida. They will amount to about 500. Col. Miller, with his officers and division, leave here forthwith for Old Point Comfort, Va., where they will be joined by others, to sail thence for Charleston, S. C. The marines from Portsmouth, Boston and New York, leave in the first packet for South Carolina. "

"NEWPORT, (R. I.) May 26.—Maj. Lomax's company of the 3d regiment U. S. artillery, which has for the last 8 or 9 years garrisoned Fort Wolcott in this harbor, embarked on Sunday last, in the steamboat Massachusetts, for New York, and left that city on Tuesday, for Charleston, on their way to Fort Mitchell, Alabama.

The promptitude displayed in moving this company, deserves notice. Major Lomax received his orders on Saturday, and on Sunday afternoon the company were on their way to New York.

We learn, that ten companies of U. S. troops, stationed along the sea-board, are ordered by the War Department, to repair to Fort Mitchell without delay .-Mercury. "

"Col. Freeman left the city yesterday with all the marines stationed at Charlestown, except a sergeant's guard, for Fort Mitchell. Lieuts. Caldwell and McArdle are of this detachment. The whole military force stationed at Fort Independence is ordered to Fort Mitchell, in Alabama, and will leave here this morning in the railroad cars for Providence. This command consists of two companies, F and K, of the second regiment of infantry. The officers are Major G. Dearborn, Major T. Staniford, Lieut G. W. Patten, and Lieut. H. W. Wessels. Orders have been received at Fort Preble, Portland, to proceed with all possible dispatch to Fort Columbus, and from thence to Fort Mitchell. Major McClintock and Capt. Vinton are of this command.—Boston Post, May 30."

"A detachment of 40 U. S. Artillery arrived in the steamboat yesterday morning from Providence; they will proceed to Fort Mitchell immediately.

A detachment of 50 Marines from the Charlestown (Mass.) navy yard are expected on here this morning in the Providence steam boat. On their arrival here, they will be joined by the marines stationed in the Navy Yard, Brooklyn, when they will proceed to Charleston immediately, thence take up their line of march for Fort Mitchell.—Ar. Y. Mer. Adv. May 31".

"THE MARINE CORPS.—The detachment of Marines, under the command of Colonel HENDERSON, which so promptly and handsomely volunteered to go against the Creek Indians, will, we understand, leave here this morning in the Columbia, for Norfolk, where they will take passage to Charleston, South Carolina, on their route to the scene of savage warfare.

This is another striking evidence of the great value of this arm of the national defense; it has shown itself as prompt to defend its country on the land as on the water, the element upon which it was designed, originally, exclusively to act. Upon several occasions during the late war with England, detachments from this brave and highly disciplined corps covered themselves with unfading laurels by their conduct while serving on land; and, in every instance of conflict on the water, its bravery and efficiency were tested by the official reports of the actions in which it bore a part.

In the present emergency it did not wait even an intimation that its services would be acceptable, but promptly came forth, through its commanding officer, in the first hour of danger, and voluntarily offered to leave their comfortable quarters, and within one week from the offer, we see a strong and well-appointed detachment of fine looking men bidding farewell to families and friends, and taking up the line of march to seek a savage and treacherous foe, in a distant land and in an inhospitable climate, to stay the ravages of war, and to protect the innocent, the helpless, and the unoffending. They will carry with them the best and warmest wishes of all, that their success may be commensurate with their bravery and zeal.

We sincerely hope this valuable corps may hereafter find that favor in the eyes of the constituted authorities of the nation, to which we think it so justly entitled.— National Intelligencer."

CHARLESTON, S, C. *June* 6.

The steam packet Columbus, Capt. HOLMES, arrived at 8 o'clock yesterday morning, having left Norfolk on Thursday evening, and having on board a large and efficient detachment of the U. S. Marine Corps, under-the immediate command of Col. HENDERSON, of that veteran body of men.

June 7.—A detachment of upwards of 300 U. S. Marines, left this city yesterday morning, on the rail road, on their way to Columbus, (Ga.) to act against the Creeks The passage money of the troops and the ordinary travelers, with their baggage, See, amounted to 82,316 38 cents.—Courier.[3]

Upon reaching Augusta Georgia, Henderson sent a dispatch to the Secretary of the Navy updating him on the progress of his troops in their movement to Columbus, Georgia.

Colonel Henderson's Report to the Secretary of the Navy

Augusta (Ga.) 9th June 1836

Sir,

I have the honor to report that the detachments of the Corps from Philadelphia, Washington and Gosport reached this city on the 7th and take up their line of march for Fort Mitchell tomorrow morning. The officers and men are generally well and I hope will go through the Campaign without much sickness.

It is however universally believed the Campaign will be short. In which case the necessity of the Corps being detained from its legitimate duties will soon cease.

I remain with gt. Respt.

Your mo. Obed. Servt.

Archibald Henderson

Colo Commt.

The Hono.

Mahlon Dickerson

Secretary of the Navy[4]

Secrecy of movements as seen above was not practiced in the press concerning the movements of troops. The Marines had made part of their movement by train, which was the first time Marines had been transported to war by train. They marched two hundred twenty-four miles from Augusta to Columbus, across Georgia in fourteen days. The arrival, personnel and mission of the Marines at Columbus, Georgia was proudly announced in the newspaper:

"From the Columbus, Georgia Sentinel, July 1st. (1836)

UNITED STATES MARINES.—The 1st battalion of U. S. Marines, under the command of Colonel Henderson, is now stationed at Camp Henderson, fifteen miles below Columbus, on the western bank of the Chattahoochee. The battalion arrived at this place on the 23d instant, having left Washington on the 1st, and Augusta on the 10th; marching from Augusta to this place in fourteen days, a distance of two hundred and twenty-four miles. On their arrival here, orders were received from General Scott to proceed to their present station with all possible dispatch, and there erect a strong picket work, as a place of deposit for provisions, Etc, for the eastern wing of the Army. Since their arrival there the officers and men have all enjoyed good health and spirits, and pursue their work with vigilance and promptness. Their location being in the most exposed part of the enemy's country; it is a great privation for them to be confined to the monotonous duties of the camp, though well convinced of the importance of their present work. Their camp has been for two successive nights roused by Indians lurking about, and approaching the picket sentinels within a few yards, when they were fired on and pursuit immediately given, but no traces of them could be found. Last night, after the roll of the drum had ceased, a whoop was distinctly heard up the river, which no doubt was a signal to a party above. On Friday morning last, a Negro boy who had escaped from the Indians that morning, and who had been a prisoner some five or six weeks, was brought into the camp by Capt. Love, of the Georgia volunteers. He stated that a party of twenty or thirty had camped the night before within six or seven miles, and had left that morning for a large swamp not far off, no doubt Cowagee swamp, and that he saw Jim Henry that day, who advised them to go as soon as possible, and that he had been badly wounded in the shoulder. Captains Twiggs and Dulany's companies, together with a company of Georgia volunteers, under Captain Love—the whole under the command of Captain Twiggs, was immediately dispatched in hopes of overtaxing them, but without success.

They soon came upon their abandoned camp, found their fires burning and meat cooking, and everything about indicating a sudden departure. A Negro man was taken in the vicinity of the camp, who, with great reluctance, gave himself up. He was armed with a musket, twenty balls, and a pocket full of powder. He was much frightened, but seemed determined to communicate as little as possible; but as far as he did tell, he corroborated the statements of the boy. The party took a number of horses belonging to the Indians, and a variety of ornaments, which they in their hurry had left behind. There is but little doubt that the Indians are concentrating somewhere in that vicinity, and will make a desperate effort to cross the river; if they do, they may be assured the troops now there will give them warm work. The following are the names of the officers now at Camp Henderson: Col. Archibald Henderson.

Lieut. Col. Samuel Miller.

Captains Levi Twiggs, John Harris, P. G. Howle, Adj't. and inspector. E. J. Weed, Major and Qr. Master, William Dulany, James McCawley.

1st Lieutenants H. N. Crabbe, A. Q. M., H. B. Tyler, G. F. Lindsay, A. C. S. 2d Battalion, F. C. Hall, F. N. Armistead, G. H. Territt, W. E. Stark.

2d Lieutenants J. T. Sprague, A. C. S.; E. L, West, W. L. Young, Josiah Watson.

Surgeon J. A. Kearney, U. S. Navy, who was attached to this battalion, has been assigned by Gen. Scott to the General Hospital in this place, and Assistant Surgeon B. Byrnes, U. S. Army, has been ordered to report to Col. Henderson for duty. Lieut. Piercy, U. S. Navy, now doing the duties of Assistant Quarter Master, has been ordered by Gen. Scott, to repair to the Head Quarters of the army in the field. The 2d battalion U. S. Marines, under the command of Lieut. Col. Freeman, is expected to arrive here on Saturday next, when they will proceed immediately to camp Henderson."[5]

Camp Henderson (near present day Cottonton) was situated on the very edge of hostile territory and as noted in the newspaper account, the camp was attacked twice at night and successfully defended by the Marines. Once situated, Lt. Colonel Samuel Miller took the First Battalion and patrolled the area at a distance of twelve miles around the camp. They did not engage the Creeks however they captured some of their women and children.

Jesup ordered Miller on July 25th to report back to Fort Mitchell from his post along the Elliot's Mail Road that he had the responsibility to protect. This was in response to an engagement between Creek warriors and two companies of Georgia volunteers who were repulsed.

From there, Miller and his troops were sent to Fort McCreary which they were to relocate the post to an area that was in a healthier place than where McCreary had been located which was considered a 'sickly location'. The new location was left to Miller's judgment as noted in General Jesup's order to him ;"*suited for defense....which at the same time promise health and afford you convenient wood and good water*".6

Companies A and B led by Captain Twiggs, searched the swamps near the camp for the Indians. One company was stationed at Upton Mills, Georgia, while the others continued patrols throughout the area all summer.

Continuous pressure from engagements with the Marines and army units wore the Creeks down at which time they surrendered. One of the groups that surrendered was captured by Henderson and a couple of his companies at Tallassee, Alabama. They kept them in a camp there until they were prepared for their relocation to the Arkansas Territory. Other groups located in the area also were escorted west, some of whom were under the command and guidance of Marine officers and men.

Miller was at West Point, Alabama with his detachment and Jesup ordered him to convene a general court martial for prisoners in his charge. He also made mention of Colonel Henderson assigning some of his officers to oversee the emigration of the Creeks. He included an order that Lt. Edson be assigned to Colonel Henderson to join those who would escort the Creeks out west. Miller was to report back to Jesup as to the disposition of the Indians in relation to both emigration and those who would volunteer to fight in Florida for his forces headed there.

From West Point, Miller was to leave only a small guard there to secure the supplies there and to take his force to the location of Tckabatchee Hajo's Camp in Chambers County, Alabama.

On September 9th, Jesup ordered Miller and his troops to the emigration camp supervised by Lt. Sprague who reported that there were about one hundred and fifty Indians hiding in the Chewarkele Swamp who refused to come in. Miller was to get them into Sprague's camp and if they refused and were hostile, to *"attack and destroy"* them. The Indians in hiding managed to evade the forces and secretly joined Sprague's group when they started out on their march west.

"FORT MITCHELL, ALABAMA,
September 12, 1836.

•*SIR: I have the honor to report, since my last communication, (August 6th,) 2,400 emigrants have been sent off in charge of Lieut. Sprague, of the U. S. Marine Corps*

All the Creek Indians are now on their way to Arkansas except the warriors who are volunteers for Florida. Their families are permitted to remain here until the campaign is over, and fed by the United States.

I have received your several communications, and will answer them shortly.

The Indian warriors are just rendezvousing at this place, preparatory for Florida.

With respect, &c.
JOHN PAGE,
Capt. Supt Creeks." [7]

Several of the Creek warriors were enlisted to join the troops who were to head to Florida to fight the Seminoles. Under their agreement, their families would be allowed to remain where they were until the services of the warriors were no longer needed, then they would be moved west to their new lands. The Creek volunteers were to receive the same pay and equipment as the soldiers, and whatever plunder they captured. They also were assured that the annuity due their people for 1837 would be paid in advance so that they were able to clear up the debts that they owed so the rest of their tribe could start the emigration to their new lands. The Creek warriors would serve under the command of Henderson and his Marines when they reached Florida.

With the removal of most of the Creek Indians at the end of the summer, Henderson took his Marines and headed south to Florida, arriving at Fort Brooke on Tampa Bay.

The emigration of the Creeks and later the Seminoles will be covered in a later chapter.

Chapter 4

Marines in the Second Seminole War 1836-1842

"Pursuant to your instructions, Lieut. Waldron, and his very effective detachment, joined this garrison on the 22nd ultimo, and has been considered so important a part of the defense as to make it necessary for them to remain............" F.S. Belton Capt. 2d Reg't Art'y Com'g

During the Second Seminole War, 1835-1842, Marines and Sailors were very much involved in fighting and gathering in Indians in Florida. The Seminoles were a collection of remnants of tribes, Lower Creeks from Georgia and Alabama (Muskogee), and Hitachi along with Yamasee, Yuchi and many runaway Negro slaves.

This war was not only about the removal of the Seminoles from Florida, but also became one for reclaiming runaway slaves from Florida. Many slaves from northern Florida and Georgia had escaped to the interior of Florida, either willingly, or as captives of the Seminoles.

These former slaves as Seminole slaves lived more freely in the Seminole settlements, having free reign of the settlement, and many owning their own cattle and crops. Others who were not slaves, blended into the settlements, intermarrying, and some even becoming leaders of their tribes.

There had been some fighting along the Florida-Georgia border prior to the war as slave hunters and owners raided Seminole settlements trying to reclaim their 'property'. In return, Seminoles would raid isolated plantations.

The fact that so many slaves had escaped to Florida and the knowledge of this spreading throughout the south, prompted slave owners to put pressure on the government to take action. Many feared the knowledge of freedom in Florida would lead to a slave revolt. These combined events are what led up to what became the longest and most expensive of the Indian Wars of this nation.

As mentioned in the previous chapter there had been several attacks by Seminoles in December 1835. This culminated in the attack on Major Dade and his command.

Major Dade, US Army, and 107 of his command were ordered to reinforce Fort King (present day Ocala). Dade and his men set out on the Fort King Military Road from Fort Brooke at Tampa Bay. They were led by a Black Seminole Indian guide named Louis Pacheco. It is still thought that Pacheco was actually allied with the attackers. Pacheco had been a slave of Antonio Pacheco, a doctor and was educated, fluent in Spanish, English and Seminole languages. When the soldiers were attacked, he quickly fled into the woods and sided with the attackers as one story goes, another indicates he was grabbed by the Indians at the start of the attack and carried off. This is the story he told for many years.

There are conflicting sources over whether Dade made the mistake of not having flankers out on the march as they moved along the road through pine forests and open grassy plains or if he did.

It was cold, and the men had their over coats on, buttoned over their cartridge boxes which would become a hindrance during the battle. About halfway between the two forts, the quiet was broken by a thunderous volley of musket fire and war whoops of the Seminoles. Almost half of the men in the column were cut down in that first volley including Dade.

In the ensuing battle, a few of the men managed to get their cannon into action, yet as the battle wore on, all the soldiers except for three were killed. Of the three, two managed to eventually escape back to Fort Brooke to tell of the massacre. The survivors told of hiding until after the battle and the following mutilation of the bodies by Black Seminoles.

This was the event that motivated the government to escalate the military presence in Florida and take the war to the Seminoles.

1836

"Our arrival was very gratifying and unexpected. We were badly needed as an attack was expected at the very time by a force of 400 Indians and their Negro allies." Lt. Waldron USMC reporting his detachment's arrival at Fort Brooke, Tampa Bay.

Fort Brooke Tampa Bay (Florida State Archives)

When word of the massacre was received at Fort Brooke, a call for help went out. The first troops to arrive to reinforce Fort Brooke were Marines. Florida Governor John Eaton ordered Master Commandant Thomas Webb of the *USS Vandalia* to send two officers along with twenty-nine Marines and sailors to patrol the coast of Florida from Pensacola to Tampa Bay in search of Indians. The settlers in Tallahassee were fearful of attacks so these men patrolled to prevent that. Their mission was accomplished without incident.

Commodore Alexander Dallas at Key West, ordered the fifty-seven Marines along with seven sailors from the *USS Constellation* and *USS St. Louis* to proceed to Fort Brooke on Tampa Bay via the merchant brig *Sunflower*. Marine Lieutenant Nathaniel Waldron commanded the Marines at Fort Brooke with the assistance of Sgt. Montgomery of the *St. Louis*.

A report from ST JOSEPH, FLORIDA INDICATED THAT *"ON JANUARY 20TH, the steam boat Eclipse, from Pensacola, touched in this harbor, on the 15th inst. with a company of Marines, from the Navy Yard at that place, under the command of Lieut. Doughty, of the U. S. Navy, on their way to Tampa Bay, to aid the suppression of the Indian hostilities. We are informed that this expedition was got up by Lieut. Goldsborough, who accompanied them, and that the boat is intended to convey soldiers up the rivers in the vicinity of the Indians."*[1]

A correspondence from the Army officer in command at Fort Brooke expressed his heartfelt thanks for the arrival of Marines:

Hon. MAHLON DICKERSON,

Secretary of the Navy,

Washington, D. C.

FORT BROOKE, TAMPA BAY, Feb. 1, 1836.

"SIR: I have the honor to acknowledge the receipt of your communication of the 17th instant, handed in by Lieutenant Waldron of the Marine Corps.

Pursuant to your instructions, Lieut. Waldron, and his very effective detachment, joined this garrison on the 22d ultimo, and has been considered so important a part of the defense as to make it necessary for them to remain, if it should meet your concurrence, until the reinforcements from New Orleans reach this place, which, if I am rightly informed, may be about the tenth instant.

But, sir, on the part of my comrades of this garrison, allow me to present to you my deep felt acknowledgments for the patriotic as well as kind feelings which conceived the possibility, and so speedily and efficiently threw into our little work a force so ready and competent to gallant achievements. A prolonged investment of this work created by daily and nightly labor, in the face of the most unflinching and martial barbarians our nation had ever struggled with, without retreat or negotiation in reserve, had tested our constancy, and daily and nightly, for weeks, every moment was expected to revenge our massacred brethren; under such circumstances, our emotion is to thank you in a tone and manner worthy of your efforts, and our responsibility to preserve this post at all hazards. I have, the honor Sec. F. S. BELTON,

Capt. 2d Reg't Art'y, Com'g."[2]

Waldron reported to a friend, *"Our arrival was very gratifying and unexpected. We were badly needed as an attack was expected at the very time by a force of 400 Indians and their Negro allies."*

Commodore Dallas was under constant pressure from the Governor of Florida and residents who constantly reported possible Indian attacks that he was kept busy supplying landing parties of his sailors and Marines along the coast between Tallahassee and St. Marks. These landing parties usually returned with no contact with the enemy. Dallas also supplied Marine guards on three steam ships that constantly navigated the Chattahoochee and Apalachicola Rivers which carried supplies and persons between Columbus Georgia and the Gulf.

In March, 1836, General Winfield Scott arrived and took command of all operations. Scott intended to attack the Seminole stronghold at the Cove of the Withlacoochee River. He set out on an operation consisting of three wings. They were all to reach their objectives by 25 March. General Clinch on the right wing would leave from Fort Drane and turn south, to prevent the Indians from moving north when pushed. The second column led by General Eustis left St. Augustine, marched along the St. John's River to Volusia, then swung west toward the Ocklawaha River then north towards the Withlacoochee to prevent the Indians from escaping to the south. The Marines under Lt. Waldron were a part of the center column, commanded by Army Colonel William Lindsey. Lindsey's column marched from Fort Brooke, up along the west side of the Withlacoochee River.

Part of Lindsey's command consisted of Alabama militia troops. They developed a great dislike for Lindsey especially when he prevented the sutlers from selling them whiskey. When they were ordered to carry their own supplies due to lack of transportation the situation grew worse. They lacked discipline and on the march they were firing at anything, so he limited their ammunition. The troops cut the mane and tail of his horse one night and after several threats, Lindsey had to be escorted by a guard detachment of Marines from the *Constellation*.

Clinch's wing only had two boats to cross the Withlacoochee, and once his troops crossed the river, they came under heavy fire and for several days fought skirmishes. They never encountered a large force of Indians by the time they reached their destination. The force under Eustis had several skirmishes with Seminoles however they too failed to engage a significant number of Indians. On March 21st Lindsey's command came under heavy fire from a thick hammock. He had his cannon brought up and when fire from that did not do much damage, he ordered a bayonet charge which drove the Indians further into the dense swamp lands.

There were no Marine casualties although two soldiers were killed and two were wounded. Due to the difficulty of transporting supplies in wagons on the poor sandy roads, all three columns ran short of rations and other supplies. By April 1st, they all headed back to their stations. Upon reaching Fort Brooke on April 4th Waldron sent his report to Commodore Dallas that: *"They suffered much fatigue and exposure and had several skirmishes with the Indians with but little loss on either side, none on the part of the Marines."*

As soon as the troops retuned to Fort Brooke, General Scott praised them and promised the volunteers that they would be sent home. However on April 9th, an Indian prisoner was brought in by one of the Revenue Cutters. He had been captured when Navy Lt. Powell of the sloop, *USS Vandalia* had sent a landing party ashore at Charlotte's Harbor due to a report of Indian hostilities at the settlement there. They built a fort large enough for them and the settlers in the area. The Indian was suspected to be one of a party that had murdered the customs agent at the settlement.

The Indian under questioning at Fort Brooke indicated that there was a large party of Indians and Negroes in the vicinity of Charlotte's Harbor and that they were well armed and had plenty of ammunition. He volunteered to guide the troops to the Indian encampment if he could gain his freedom in return. General Smith of the volunteers offered to take his men and chase down the Indians. Weary though they were from the battle and march from the Wahoo Swamp, they set out on the brigantine *Calvin* and sloop *Cumberland* and reached Charlotte's Harbor where they were met by Lt. Powell and the landing party of sailors and Marines.

They set out marching from the mouth of the Myakka River where they had left a store of supplies. After the first day's march, many of the soldiers were too worn out, from the constant exertions their uniforms and shoes in tatters. Those who could not continue, General Smith let return to their supply camp. The rest managed to set forth up the Myakka, some in canoes, others on foot.

The two parties met up the next day and set all set out in canoes, Lt. Powell heading one column, and Captain Ross the other. The men were awe struck by the beauty of the deep river, the forests and the rich fertile land around it. There was plenty of game along the river and an abundance of fish seen swimming along the way. It was no wonder the Indians longed to stay in this area. They camped the next night and on the 20th, had to leave their canoes as the river was full of obstructions and shouldering their packs, set out through the woods guided by their captive. They came across many tracks and recent campfires. That night they camped at an old Indian encampment, and made shelters of palmetto fronds to shelter themselves from the rain. They called the place 'Cowpens' as there was a large cattle pen there which had been built by the Indians. They struck out the next day crossing a couple of prairies however they never found any of the enemy.

The expedition returned down river and joined those who had been waiting at the mouth of the Myakka on the 23rd. They then boarded the ships and reached Fort Brooke on the 27th.

Also on May 2, 1836, Lt. Ellison of the *USS Concord* was ordered to patrol south of Fort Brooke to the mouth of the Manatee River and the islands at the mouth of the harbor (bay). He was to take the launch of the *USS Concord*, one midshipman, sixteen men to include a corporal and two Marines. They covered that area, including Bunce's new Rancho (Captain William Bunce had several 'fishing ranchos' along the coast which traded their catches in Cuba), Egmont Key, Passage Key and then to Mullet Key. There they were met by the Revenue cutter *Washington* and towed back to Fort Brooke.

This was a reconnaissance patrol to.. *"ascertain if there are any Indians in that vicinity, which you will be able to do from their tracks, smoke, etc...."* as directed by Captain Mervine Mix. They were further instructed to *"Keep your howitzer at all times loaded as well as your small arms, and be at all times prepared to operate against any force that the enemy may bring against you."* [3] The men found no Indians on their patrol after four days of searching.

On May 9th, Lt Howard was ordered to patrol ten miles south of Sarasota Island to Stoney Point to investigate the report of twenty-five canoes of hostile Indians. His command consisted of the launch with twenty-three officers, crew and Marines along with the first cutter manned by eighteen officers, seaman and Marines. The launch was armed with a twelve pound howitzer, and each man was armed with a musket, pistol and cutlass. They were supplied with enough provisions for a week. They returned on May 13th reporting that the canoes seen by the transport ship that reported them belonged to the people of Charlotte's Harbor who relocated to Bunce's Rancho at the entrance of the bay there.

Captain Mix of the *Concord* in late May had determined it would be necessary to remain at Tampa Bay with the Marines ashore at Fort Brooke to bolster the force there. He lists the total troop force at Fort Brooke as two hundred and seventeen including the Marines.

Further south the Navy and Marines patrolled around south Florida. Besides protecting settlers they were also to disrupt trade between the Indians and Cubans. Many Cuban fishermen set up fish camps along the coast of Florida and traded liquor and weapons to the Indians for their goods. Navy Lt. Powell built a small supply depot on Key Biscayne after the attack on the lighthouse and a fort at the south side of the mouth of the Miami River and called it Fort Dallas after the Commodore of the West Indies Squadron.

Lt Powell along with his sailors and his twenty Marines patrolled the area. Marines also manned a small fort on the Miami River named Fort Kemble. From there they protected wood cutting parties sent out by the ships on patrol. Indians were raiding settlements and had driven several settlers into the Keys, many of whom joined the settlement on Indian Key.

On July 24th, 1836, Marines and sailors on board the transport schooner *Motto* made a rescue of an unusual nature. Lt. Leib of the *USS Concord* at Tampa Bay, had been ordered to take the ship and his twenty Marines to Key West to deliver two pieces of ordnance, then to Indian Key to determine if it would be necessary to leave the Marines under Sgt. Wright there for their defense. Then they were to proceed to the location of the wreck of the *Gil Blas* near New River as it was believed that there was a shipment of lead on board the wreck that the Indians might discover.

They reached Key West on the 16th of July. They were detained briefly at Indian Key due to damage to the rudder, and determined that the Marines would not be needed there. They did not arrive at the wreck of the *Gil Blas* until the 24th. By diving into the wreck they discovered no lead there, so they set the wreckage on fire. That night they discovered the fire at the lighthouse.

John Thompson keeper of the Cape Florida lighthouse on Key Biscayne and his helper, were set upon by a band of Seminoles. They managed to barricade themselves in the lighthouse while the Indians plundered and set fire to the out buildings. When they tried to breakdown the lighthouse door, Thompson fired down on them from a window. When darkness fell, the Indians snuck back to the lighthouse door and set it on fire. The fire reached lamp oil stored on the first floor, which in turn set the wood staircase leading to the top of the structure on fire. Thompson and his assistant by that time were at the very top by the lantern. Grabbing an axe, he headed back down the staircase and started hacking away at the lower staircase with his axe until the flames got to be too much for him.

The flames shot up the tower, and exploded when it reached the lantern, lighting up the night sky as the entire staircase, and lantern oil burned fiercely. The two men lay on the small platform to prevent the Indians from shooting them. In desperation, Thompson dropped his keg of gunpowder down into the flames, causing a loud explosion.

The Indians surmised that the two men died in the explosion and left the island taking their loot and Thompson's boat. The explosion was heard by the crew of the *Motto* a few miles out to sea and the Marine private on watch spied the flames.

The next day after working in through the reefs, Captain Armstrong sent two boats of Marines and sailors ashore under the command of Lt. Lloyd. The landing party secured the area, and set out to try and rescue the light keeper from the top of the tower. He had been shot in both feet, and burned. His Negro assistant succumbed to his wounds during the night and died.

The sailors tried to hoist a line to the top by use of a kite; however the prevailing winds did not cooperate. Finally one of the Marines tied string to his ramrod, dropped it in the barrel of his musket and fired it over the top of the tower. Thompson was able to pull the string which had a rope and tackle attached and secured it to the top of the tower. Two sailors hoisted themselves up and were able to lower the man to the beach. They took him to the hospital at Key West where he recovered from his wounds. Leib and his command returned from his mission on August 5th. He reported, *"The officers, Seamen and Marines acquitted themselves to my satisfaction."*5

Commodore Dallas moved his broad pennant from the *Constellation* at Pensacola to the *Concord* at Tampa Bay. In his December 13th, 1836 report to General Jesup, he stated that "The number of Seamen and Marines whom I can place in active cooperation with you will be nearly 400." He also reported that a party of 150 Seamen and Marines had been patrolling to the south from New River and Cape Florida to Charlotte Harbor, as well as entering fifteen miles into the Everglades, and had discovered no Indians

Escalation: The Marine Regiment Arrives

"October 28ᵗʰ... in the course of the day the Marines landed. They are in good order and fully provided with comfortable tents....." Lt. Henry Prince

After their fighting Creek Indians in Georgia and Alabama during the summer of 1836, Henderson and the regiment arrived at Fort Brooke in October. Once there, they relieved the Marines of the West India Squadron, who returned to their ships. Army Lt. Henry Prince who was stationed at Fort Brooke, noted in his diary; *"October 28ᵗʰ... in the course of the day the Marines landed. They are in good order and fully provided with comfortable tents. October 30ᵗʰ Colonel Henderson takes command of all the troops at this post. He outranks everything below the General."* (From the book, *Amidst a Storm of Bullets, The Diary of Lt. Henry Prince in Florida*). Prince also noted in his journal, that Colonel Henderson had the nickname of *"Old Piss to Windward".*[6]

During the remainder of 1836 and 1837, the Marines' duties were twofold. For the first few months, Henderson was given command of Fort Brooke and Tampa Bay. Some of his men took up regular patrols, and manned a few of the forts, while others escorted wagon trains of supplies between the forts, freeing up soldiers for duty with the rest of the army.

When Jesup was ready to mount major operations in the field, he gave Henderson command of the Second Brigade which was composed of most of the Marines, mounted and un-mounted, Creek Indian volunteers and Alabama Militia. He gave command of Tampa Bay, Fort Brooke, troops stationed there along with one company of Marines to Henderson's second in command, Lt. Col. Samuel Miller. He was to oversee the area, logistics, and security of the surrounding area and eventually the encampment of Indians as they came in to surrender.

To keep continuity in respect to the two separate duties, I am separating the two here. This next section will cover the support duties and that will be followed by the field service.

Support Duties

"The devotion which you have on all occasions evinced for the service, and the energy and promptitude with which you have performed every duty which has devolved on your merits the highest commendations, and I applaud you Colonel, that I will always retain the most grateful recollections of your service." Lt General Thomas Jesup to Marine Lt. Col Samuel Miller January 20ᵗʰ, 1837

While Henderson was still in charge of Tampa Bay between October and December 1836, General Jesup concerned about the ammunition, ordered Henderson to assemble a board for the purpose of experimenting to determine if they could effectively reduce the amount of powder per round, and achieve a satisfactory result. Henderson's board recommended a slight reduction of powder per round on the 15ᵗʰ of November.

On the 10ᵗʰ of November, Jesup ordered Henderson to have a schooner search the area for liquor as many of the workmen and soldiers were turning up drunk. Lt Chambers was also ordered to go back north due to his ill health. Jesup gave orders to Henderson to release the soldiers held as prisoners at Fort Brooke except for one who had attempted to kill another soldier and return them to work. Any able bodied man who would not work would not be offered rations.

In December, Miller took over Fort Brooke and Tampa Bay. One of the first assignments he was given was the supplying the fort being rebuilt at the site of old Fort Alabama. He and Lt. Colonel Freeman kept the Marines and artillerists constantly on the move guarding the wagon trains of supplies to the fort site twenty four miles north of Tampa.

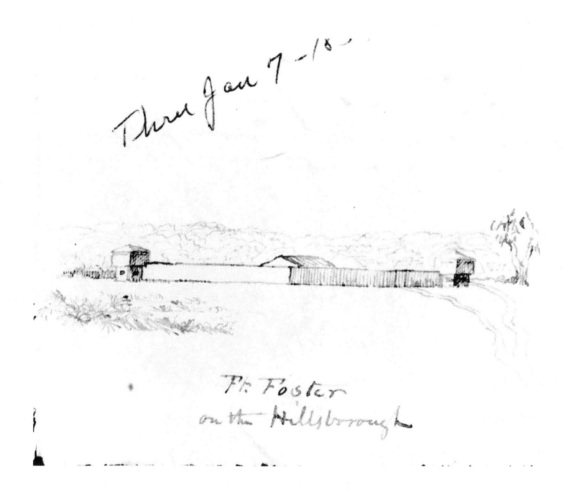

Fort Foster as drawn by Lt. Henry Prince U.S. Army (picture from University of Florida)

Army Colonel William S. Foster was ordered to rebuild the bridge over the Hillsborough River and the fort where the former Fort Alabama stood along the Fort King Road. The fort had been abandoned earlier, and when the troops left it bringing out their supplies, they left several kegs of gunpowder in the magazine, rigged with a musket and line tied to the door. When the troops were less than a mile away, they heard a tremendous explosion, caused by the Seminoles entering the fort.

It was necessary to reestablish this fort along the Fort King Road between Fort Brooke on Tampa Bay, and Fort King (where Ocala is now). This would provide protection for the bridge and also be a supply depot for the troops operating in the field. Foster and his men arrived at the location on December 1st and started work the next day, with the work parties being covered by a strong guarding force.

Foster kept a journal of the time spent there and noted the participation of the Marines supplying them.

"December 4th. Sunday. The Parties reorganized and at work. At 5PM, Col. Freeman arrived with 200 troops consisting of Marines, Artillery & 20 friendly Indians, for the purpose of conveying back the baggage wagons, 16 in number & Artillery Horses."

"December 8th. Thursday. Weather continues cool, frost last night. Our Block Houses and Pickets present an imposing view against Indians. At 7 o'clock this evening Col. Freeman of the Marine Corps arrived with the convoy & baggage train & one piece of Artillery for the Block House. The escort consisted of 200 men, Marines & Artillery & 21 wagons loaded with provisions and Qtr. Master Stores, left Tampa at 8 AM."

"December 9th. Friday. Clear & pleasant. The wagons being unloaded, Col. Freeman & Guard left this at 8AM this morning for Tampa Bay, taking with them the 24 empty wagons and three carts. Parties still at work at the Block Houses, setting Pickets &c., most of the logs are upon the 2nd story. A party detailed to pitch a Marquee to store the provisions, under the direction of the Ast. Com. Sub. Lt. Wall."

"Dec. 13th. Tuesday. Warm & sultry, the wind blowing from the south, flying clouds, with the appearance of rain shortly. From 125 to 150 men are daily employed at the different works. At 12 M the wind shifted to the Southwest and blew in gusts during the afternoon. At 4 PM the Recall sounded to discontinue work. High winds & some rain. Sunset, the storm continues & beyond a doubt we shall pass an uncomfortable night. A wolf trap set but a pen would by far be preferable. Commenced covering our Store House today.

Sunset. Our wagons loaded with provisions & corn are in sight, 25 in number. The Guard Consisting of about 200 Marines & Artillery with a Howitzer, commanded by Col. Freeman, M. Corps in person (appears much fatigued having been in movement since 2 o'clock this morning. The distance from this place to Fort Brooke in Tampa is at least 24 miles, making a great days march for loaded wagons.) There is now at this Post, at the lowest computation, 35,000 rations. The field report of this day is, Effective 311, Rank & File. Men, Aggregate 334."

"December 14th. Wednesday. Clear and serene, pleasant fine weather. Our Store House not being finished, obliged to pitch another Marquee to store the provisions. The ration of Bread & Bacon is of an indifferent quality, many worms in the bread from age & the bacon rank and stale. Capt. G.W.Allen of the 4th Infty took with him the companies "A', "D" & "K" of the 4th, & armed, crossed the Hillsborough River, and having thrown out a covering party commenced opening the road from the site of the bridge to intersect the old Road. Additional party detailed to assist the Pickets & Qtr. Masters works. The Carpenters at work at the gates. The Guard occupies Block House No. 1 upon the right. The Guard to the wagons & teams are allowed this day for rest. The principle Engineer, Lt. Prince, is busily employed at the works."

"Dec. 15th. Thursday. Clear and warm, & pleasant. Col. Freeman with the Guard and wagons departed at daylight this morning for Tampa. Maj. McClintock with the most of three Companies of Artillery crossed the river & continued at cutting and opening the Hammock in front of the works, a Sergt. And Corp. from the Infantry obtaining leave to visit Tampa & return with the next convoy. Our Store House is now in situation to received supplies. Party by detail at work cutting brush & undergrowth, piling and burning, so as [to] have a view into the Hammock opposite the works."

"Dec.17th.Saturday. Morning, damp &chilly, considerable rain having fallen before daylight this morning, distant heavy thunder. High winds at 10 AM from the North. The parties still at work, a part of

the E duty men policing around the Pickets & Block Houses, some work done to the floors at Block House

No. 1. Pioneers and a party at work on the opposite side of the river. The Pickets completed.

Order No. 7. The men are directed to discontinue work on tomorrow. It being Sunday, they will be

allowed the day for cleaning themselves after having discharged their pieces and cleaned them. (At 1 PM)

the Van Guard appeared in sight followed by 26 wagons loaded with provisions, escorted by 200 men,

Artillery & Marines, commanded by Col. Miller, with a Six Pounder. Our front gate, a large double one

admitting a wagon team was this day hanged upon its hinges. Some port holes cut in the Pickets &

shutters for ports in the Block Houses made. There has been no idling of time from the 1ˢᵗ inst. To the

present date, our little Fort presents a neat & clean appearance. The opening of the Hammock has added

much to the prospect."

"December 18ᵗʰ. Sunday. Chilly & cold, the air very sharp in the fore part of the day. Wind from the

north. Assembly beat at 8 AM to discharge our pieces by companies, under the direction of Company

Officers to report the 1ˢᵗ & 2ⁿᵈ best shots in each company and the men to receive an extra Gill of liquor.

Distance 100 yds.. The troops returned to camp, cleaned their arms and themselves & allowed the rest of

the day for rest as also the guard from Tampa with the wagons after storing the provisions in the Ast.

Com. store house....."

"December 19ᵗʰ. Monday. Cloudy. The Guard & wagons departed at daylight this morning for Tampa,

Capt. P. Morrison accompanied them......"

"December 20ᵗʰ. Tuesday. Cloudy, some rain in the morning. Two regular officers, Lts. Bainbridge and

Wagner & 2 Indians arrived from Gen. Jesup's camp at 12 last night (who proceeded on to Tampa

without delay) and at sunrise this morning two volunteers of the Alabama Corps arrived Express with

such information as induced Col. Foster to send out wagons, the Actg. Adj. Lt. Prince, a Corp. & 4 men immediately to Tampa with advices to Col. Henderson's Marine Corps of the situation of Gen. Jesup's army & Genl. Armstrong. The two officers last spoken of also left this for Tampa Bay at the same time."7

Foster and his men completed the fort including the two blockhouses within 18 days. The fort was named Fort Foster in his honor. While some of his men were left to complete the work on the bridge, Foster and part of his command left to commence work on Fort Dade on the Withlacoochee River to the north on December 22nd.

Fort Foster was now equipped with one six-pounder and one howitzer with 100 rounds for each. At least 25,000 ball-and buckshot cartridges, with 25,000 rounds of rifle powder were also stored there. The fort was stocked with 50,000 rations and 10,000 bushels of corn, along with tools, rope and nails for maintenance of the fort and bridge. He was to stock Fort Dade with at least as much.

Rations in those days included pork, bacon, salt, fresh beef (plentiful in Florida thanks to the early Spanish settlers in the 1600's), vinegar, pickles, cucumbers, onions, cabbage, and bread.

Foster reported that they had only advanced 4 miles across the river when they met the advance party of General Jesup's command. It included about 400 Alabama volunteers, some Regulars and Marines, all mounted and 'much fatigued' headed for Tampa Bay.

Army Major W. L. McClintock left in charge of the work party at Foster, reported another convoy brought by Marine Col. Freeman, *"Freeman being in a great hurry as usual."8*

December 26th, Foster reported a convoy of 37 wagons & 6 carts with provisions and forage accompanied by 100 Marines, arriving at his position at the Withlacoochee River where they were building the fort and bridge. Next to arrive on the same day was a convoy of 110 pack horses, each loaded with 4 bushels of corn led by Col. Freeman with 40 Alabama volunteers and 40-50 mounted Marines as guards. The next day Freeman proceeded to Fort Armstrong with half of the load of corn.

Foster's last mention of the Marines was on December 29th when he reported that Colonel Freeman on his return from Fort Armstrong, took with him 39 wagons, 6 carts and all the pack horses along with his Marine guard and returned to Tampa Bay. He also was accompanied by Doctor Abadie of the Marine Corps.

January 1st, 1837, General Jesup was preparing to take to the field in pursuit of the Seminoles with Colonel Henderson's Marines and other troops so Lt. Col. Miller was left in charge at Fort Brooke and surrounding Tampa Bay area.

Miller was to take charge of the post until a naval garrison arrived to take over. His duties included manning the fort, overseeing the arrival and equipping arriving troops, seeing to the protection of the cattle herd kept across the Hillsborough River from the fort, and protecting the supply wagon trains sent to the troops in the field and the other forts. Later he also over saw the placement of the Indians who came in after the cessation of hostilities in preparation for emigration to the west.

"Your command will be one company of Marines, the convalescents and the troops employed in the service staff departments." As noted by Jesup in his order to Miller.[9]

Miller was to remain at Fort Brooke after the naval garrison arrived to oversee the arrival of the 6th regiment of the Army, then with his Marines and whatever of the convalescents who had recovered and bring them to Jesup in the field. A dispute between Miller and Army Major Thompson as to who had the right to command as Thompson believed that he should be in command over the Marine Lt. Colonel. Jesup did not want to have a dispute of this type arising at the beginning of his campaign, so he ordered Major Thompson to join him in the field which would leave Miller in charge at Fort Brooke.

On January 20th, Jesup instructed Miller to accept two battalions of Alabama troops at the fort as part of his command so that his Marines could take the field. He was to *'make the Alabama troops as useful as possible'*. Miller was to send his Marines and the artillery guard at Fort Foster to Jesup as soon as a guard of Marines from the naval detachment could relieve the men at Fort Foster. He addressed Miller in this order *as 'Lt. Colonel Samuel Miller, Commanding Escort & the forts on the route to Fort Armstrong'*.

On February 9th, Jesup communicated to Miller the cessation of hostilities after the battle of Hatchee Lustee, with the promise of the main chiefs to communicate with their people and meet with the General at Fort Dade on February 18th. He sent the Indian Jim Boy, a volunteer Creek Indian to him who was to be under Miller's command. At the same time he expressed his regrets for the deaths of wagon master McDuff and private Pleasants, hoping that their unfortunate demise would serve as an example to others not to wander too far from the garrison without sufficient guard.

Marine Captain Harris' company and the warriors of Chief Cochus Micco and Echo Hadjo accompanied a wagon train from Fort Dade on February 21st with the instructions of keeping the friendly Indians at Tampa Bay as long as a sufficient guard could be sent back with the new wagon train of supplies as Harris' men were to return immediately. These Indians were to remain there to avoid conflicts with the Seminoles as they were surrendering. They were promised the plunder that they could take, so with the Seminoles giving up, there was temptation for the volunteers to take what they could from the defeated Seminoles.

In March, Miller set the Alabama troops busy improving the road from Fort Brooke to the Little Hillsborough River (today's by-pass canal). On the 11th, Miller received word from Jesup that Chief To-Lak Coo Chee (Cloud) would be bringing his people to Tampa Bay in preparation for emigration to the west. Miller was to locate them in a camp near Dickson's Settlement seven or eight miles from Fort Brooke on the Indian River (in the vicinity of today's Orient Road Jail) and provide them with subsistence sugar and coffee rations and whatever supplies that they needed.

On the 20th a Marine noncom and four privates arrived at Fort Brooke with Indian prisoners. The Marines were not able to relax at the fort as the next day they had to return to Fort Dade.

Miller received instructions from Jesup on the March 27 to investigate Mr. Cooley who had arrived at Tampa Bay with suspicious motives. He had at one point been the light house keeper at Biscayne Bay, and lost his family to the Indian attacks. Cooley was at Tampa to try to round up Black Seminoles to return to slave owners if he could get them away from the encampment at Tampa Bay. He had been trying to spread rumors among those gathering for emigration, that some of the Seminoles were going to head into the Everglades. He had hoped that some of the Black Seminoles would then slip away so that he and his men could capture them away from the troops. Cooley was eventually ordered from the area.

June 12th, Jesup requested Miller to have Freeman and his command to continue in their patrols rather than to be assigned to wagon train escorts.

June 25th, Jesup sent orders to Miller that the Creek Indian Volunteers were to be kept patrolling around the area to be watchful for the enemy. Some of them were to join the cattle guard across the Hillsborough River also. He was to also ensure the safety of the wagon trains of supplies between Tampa Bay and Fort Dade. Miller was to have a hospital constructed on one of the keys in the bay (most likely a small key just north of Mullet Key long since washed away by storms). The Spanish of the fishing rancho were to be employed to build the hospital and out buildings. Jesup stressed that, *"The utmost vigilance must on all occasions be observed and care must be taken to prevent the escape of the prisoners. Should the enemy be observed in the neighborhood of the fort, all the Indian Negroes in camp must be placed within the pickets, and as soon as possible be sent to New Orleans, to the Quartermaster there who will either secure them at the barracks or send them to Fort Pike".*

Jesup closed this order expressing his confidence in Miller, *"Placing every _____ Colonel, on your energy, vigilance and capacity, I commit the direction of the service and the defense of the post and harbor to you, with perfect confidence that whatsoever may be necessary will be done under any circumstances that may arise and I have the honor to be,*

Most respectfully,

Your Obt. Servt.

T S Jesup

Major General Comd." [10]

Writing from St Augustine where Jesup was laid up due to an injury to his ankle, he cautioned Miller about some of the Chiefs that were there at Tampa Bay. *"Bowlegs is an important person-keep him securely and allow no discourse with him. Abraham and Toney as well as Bob, must be closely watched".* Some of the other Indians were having second thoughts about their agreement to emigrate. If such Indians came around that were not willing to emigrate, *"Abraham and Toney will take the first opportunity to leave us. If they have not already been placed within the pickets, I wish you to secure them, also Bob, should any Indian signs be discovered in the neighborhood."* [11]

Miller continued to command the troops at Tampa Bay until he left for the north. From that time, Captain William Dulaney was in command of the remaining Marines who performed duty in the field with Jesup.

Duties in the Field

Marines and Creek volunteers led by Marine officers participated in a raid on the Wahoo Swamp. During the battle Lt. Andrew Ross was mortally wounded and died of his wounds days later, the first Marine to die in Florida and the first Marine officer to be killed since the War of 1812.

"DEATH OF LIEUT. ROSS OF THE MARINE Corps. —It is our melancholy duty to state that this gallant officer who was wounded on the 21st ult. while leading his men over a creek in the Wahoo Swamp, under a heavy fire of the enemy, is no more. He reached Fort Heileman on the 2d inst., and died on the 10th. Every kindness was extended to him, and his Surgeon writes that he bore his sufferings with heroic fortitude. He was to have been buried on the 11th with the honors of war. We truly sympathize with the wife of his bosom, and young children, who reside in our borough, in this hour of their trial.—Norfolk Beacon. "[12]

Marines of the West Indies Squadron were busy during this period also. Navy Lt. Levin M. Powell was credited with the concept of Riverine Warfare during this period. When he was reassigned to other duties, Lt. John McLaughlin expanded the concept which helped speed the end of the war.

Powell had early experience working with Army Colonel Smith at Charlotte's Harbor on a foray inland. Later in October 1836, he was assigned to take a naval force of sailors and all the Marines of the squadron except for a small detachment on board the *St. Louis*, from Pensacola to Key West. Reports from captured Seminoles placed a force of Indians gathering at the Pease River on the west coast moving south, and another large group operating in the vicinity of Cape Florida and New River on the east coast.

Marine First Lt. Waldron was in charge of the Marines. He already had experience fighting Seminoles after his detachment had been landed at Fort Brooke earlier that year. He and his Marines had several skirmishes with the hostiles. Powell's detachment was accompanied by Naval Lt. William Smith and Surgeon Hassler, both of whom already had some experience in previous small boat expeditions. Guiding them were two civilians. Steven Mallory of Key West, who in later years became the secretary of the navy for the Confederacy. He was joined by Dr. Frederick Leitner who had spent time in Southern Florida studying the flora and fauna of the region.

The force was transported on the *USS Vandalia* and the Revenue Cutter *Washington*. The sailors and Marines would patrol using the *Washington* as a floating base and the smaller schooner boats *Firefly* and *Carolina* for patrol. The force consisted of ninety-five Marines and fifty sailors.

Powell's force left Key West headed for Cape Florida on October 3rd, stopping at Indian Key for water. There they learned that a force of Seminoles had attacked Key Largo the previous day, destroying several buildings of the lighthouse keeper. They had also attacked a schooner anchored at Key Tavernier. They set the ship on fire after taking all they could from it. The crew had escaped in the ship's boats although two were wounded in the escape. Cruising the coast, Powell's force spotted the camp fires of the raiding party and set out to ambush them. His plan to get between the Indians and the mainland did not pan out although they did spot two Indians in a canoe and gave chase.

The Indians had the advantage of being in shallower water and led the sailors and Marines on until they reached a spot where they went ashore and ran off. Powell put a landing party ashore. They found an abandoned village that the Indians managed to reach in time to warn the occupants. The landing party burned the village, canoes and everything that they found there.

Powell then directed Lt. Smith to take their larger vessels ahead to Cape Florida while he and the Marines went on in the smaller boats to search the area between Key Largo and the mainland, finally reaching Cape Florida on the 21st.

From their base there, Powell sent out scouting parties to search for any Indian sign. Lt. Smith with the sailors went to the Miami River to search around an old village, while Lt. Waldron and the Marines rowed up the Miami River as far as they could go in their boats. All that they found there were villages that had been previously abandoned and burnt.

The next area that Powell decided to search was along New River where it was known that the Seminoles harvested coontie. He chose to use a two-pronged approach. He sent Lt. Smith to approach the mouth of the river by sea, while he and the Marines were to head up to the headwaters of the Ratones River, and from there, they were to march over land to New River. Once there, they would descend the river until they met with Smith's party.

Powell's force rowed all night and reached the Ratones the next morning at 10:00 am. They then marched eight miles over land to reach New River, torching an abandoned village along the way.

Satisfied that the Seminoles had left the area to go north, Powell, after making a brief excursion into the Everglades, decided to end the expedition and return the men to their commands. Marines were sent back to Tampa Bay, most of them arriving on the schooner *Dexter* early in December.

On November 29th, Jesup set out with a company of mounted Marines and Lt. Col Caulfield's battalion to meet up with General Call at Volusia. They camped at Lake Thonotosassa fifteen miles from Fort Brooke. They continued on to the remains of old Fort Alabama, which Jesup ordered Colonel Foster to rebuild (he renamed this Fort Foster in January). They journeyed on, crossing both branches of the Withlacoochee. They discovered shacks, cattle, Indian and horse tracks, and finally camped at the site of Dade's massacre. Here they rounded up some cattle and had fresh meat.

They continued on until they reached Palalikaha where they came across an encampment of Tennesseans and friendly Indians. There had been a large number of dead horses nearby as the volunteers' mounts had played out. On the 3rd of December, they captured an Indian after crossing the Ocklawaha. He agreed to lead Lt. Col. Caulfield and two companies to a nearby Negro village. Late that night, Caulfield and his command returned to Jesup's camp with forty one prisoners. The troops managed to surprise the village, which they destroyed after allowing the prisoners to gather their belongings.

On December 4th, they met up with Governor Call near the St. John's River. Call had some regular troops, Tennessee volunteers and friendly Creek warriors. They were in the process of building a fortification at Volusia to house supplies. The Governor believed the Seminoles were headed back to the Withlacoochee although the General was not in agreement. Call turned over his troops to Jesup, and once the fortification (named Fort Call) was complete and supplies gathered in, Jesup started out with Harris' mounted Marines, Alabama mounted volunteers and Tompkins' artillery headed for the Ocklawaha. Here the Florida and Alabama volunteers captured a hundred head of cattle.

Lt Caulfield's troops had detached to attack the village of Chief Osuchee, known also as Cooper. They managed to burn the village, and the only occupant was an aged Negro, whom they did not bother to take prisoner. By the 17th, the troops reached Dade's battleground and camped. Indian scouts were sent into the Wahoo Swamp and the Cove of the Withlacoochee to search for signs of the Seminoles.

The scouts discovered only trails heading to the south east with no Seminoles remaining in the area. Jesup sent the Tennessee volunteers back to Fort Brooke as their terms of service were expiring. He received word from Colonel Henderson at Fort Brooke that Commodore Dallas had arrived, so Jesup set out for Tampa Bay with his Marines to meet with him. Dallas agreed to spare men of the fleet to man Fort Brooke and Fort Foster. Jesup also asked for and Dallas agreed to keep a ship patrolling around the mouth of the Withlacoochee River.

1837

"Camp Hillsborough 7 miles from Tampa

13ᵗʰ April 1837

"The Indians come in slowly, but such is their characteristic, & I doubt not they will all be in this month or early in the next. We expect the first emigrating party to start the last of this week." Archibald Henderson's report on the surrendering Seminoles.

January 1837 proved to be a busy month for the Marines. Sixty Marines from the squadron were sent up the Clear River (possibly the Anclote) twenty miles north of Tampa Bay to search for Indians. The Marines under Henderson undertook a major operation with General Jessup.

On January 3ʳᵈ, Jesup and the troops marched out from Fort Brooke along with Henderson and his Marines, meeting up at Fort Foster the next day. Here, Jesup reorganized the troops into two brigades, giving Henderson command of the 2ⁿᵈ brigade.

On January 6ᵗʰ, 1837, the General took the mounted Marines to Fort Armistead, to assist in the dismantling of that fort and retrieval of the supplies there. During this month of patrols the Marines under Henderson captured 24 saddles, 3 canoes, 24 ponies, 306 head of cattle, 6 horses and 24 mules.

On January 10ᵗʰ, Jesup joined Henderson and his five hundred troops and proceeded to the Panasofkee Swamp where they camped. They searched the surrounding area. Henderson took on the infantry, baggage wagons, mounted troops and Indian volunteers and proceeded through the swamps searching the area as they went by the 19ᵗʰ.

On the 23rd, Lt. Col. Caulfield was detached with his battalion and Harris' Mounted Marines to attack Chief Philip and his Negro band on Lake Apopka. They met back up with Jesup after successfully surprising Chief Cooper, killing him and capturing nine Indians and eight Negros.

On the 27th, Jesup detached Colonel Henderson with Caulfield's and Harris' mounted men along with Morris' Indian warriors. Marine Captain Delany and troops were sent in another direction following tracks into a swamp. Henderson sent back word that they had captured one hundred head of cattle and were pursuing tracks. A small guard was left with the cattle to guard it. Jesup continued to follow Henderson's brigade, crossing the Thlassee Hatchee creek where he made camp, leaving Marine Lt. Colonel Freeman in charge.

Jesup had the other detachments called back to the camp, then proceeded to try to catch up with Colonel Henderson's brigade as they were moving fast in pursuit. Henderson was at least four miles in advance of Jesup's men and had attacked through a small village. When Jesup got there it was too dark to continue and had his men return to camp. Later that night, Henderson and his men came in with twenty-eight Indian and Negro prisoners.

Henderson's unit had met up with Seminoles in the swampy area of the Hatchee-Lustee River (now called Reidy Creek near Disney World). The Marines and Alabama troops surprised some Seminoles. The warriors caught by surprise fled into the Big Cypress Swamp, there at Hatchee-Lustee Creek, the Seminoles made their stand.

Henderson divided his troops into three units, two of which were deployed to set up crossfire on the opposite bank of the creek. The creek was deep and about 25 yards across. There were two felled trees across it for "bridges" Captain John Harris commanding the Horse Marines, led the third unit across the trees at which point the Seminoles fled deeper into the swamp. There firefights between the Indians and the Marines followed with the Seminoles falling still further back and out of the swamp into a stand of pines.

The Marine officers led the charge. Captain Morris, Lt. Chambers, and Lt. Searle. Captain Morris and Lt. Lee led the charge across the creek, followed by their men. Private Wright was killed crossing; Sgt. Cunningham, and Privates Sullivan and Foley were wounded. As the fight continued, Private Peterson and Corporal Stevens were wounded.

A few Seminoles and Black Seminoles were killed by Henderson's men but 6 Marines were killed, two outright and four later dying of their wounds. They captured twenty-eight Seminoles and Black Seminoles, mostly women and children; however most of the Seminoles' worldly goods were captured, packed on the one hundred ponies that the troops captured.

This seemed to have a strong impact on the Seminoles, and especially Chief Abraham. The Indian Chiefs agreed to parley within the next couple of months. On the morning of the 28th, a prisoner was sent to find Chief Jumper to ask for a parlay to discuss surrender. The messenger returned on the 29th with a response from Alligator and Abraham, who agreed to meet. Captain Harris and his Marines kept on the patrol in the direction that Abraham's people had retreated.

Abraham came into the camp on the 31st, and met with Jesup. He indicated that he, Alligator and Jumper desired peace. Jumper was ill and could not come in at the moment; however he was in agreement to be moved west. The three chiefs told Jesup that it was the Miccosukees who had caused the war and had convinced the Seminoles to join in with them.

The chiefs let Jesup know that if Micanopy agreed to go west, they would convince their people to move also. Abraham returned to his people accompanied by Harris' mounted Marines to protect him from the friendly Indians on patrol. Henderson's actions throughout the Big Cypress area for the past two months kept the Seminoles on the move which helped wear them out.

On February 3rd, General Jesup with Harris' Marines as an escort with several of his officers crossed the Thlassee Hatchee and met with the chiefs who had agreed to meet with them. Once they gathered, the Indians seemed nervous of having so many mounted men, that Jesup had his escort return to camp. After much discussion they agreed to meet again on the 18th at Fort Dade, to give the chiefs time to round up all their people as they had spread out around mid- Florida.

On the 9th of February, Jesup ordered that the 2nd brigade to return to Fort Dade in preparation for the assembly of the Indians, and to keep patrols around the area. Slowly the chiefs came in; first Abraham on the 21st, then a few days later, Cloud and Alligator followed by Holach Touchee and Micanopy several days later. They agreed to meet at Tampa Bay in late March.

Also during the months of January through March, Marines from the West Indies Squadron were involved in actions. On January 1st, 1837, Lt Leib of the *USS Concord* along with two midshipmen and sixty-one men were assigned to Fort Foster for its defense while the soldiers moved on up the road where Foster was to erect another fort.

At the same time another naval party was assigned to man Fort Clinch at the mouth of the Withlacoochee. Lt. Bell, boarded the steamship *American* with two midshipmen, thirty-seven sailors and the following Marines; Sgt John Montgomery, Corporal Joseph Lyons, Privates D. Morrison, Hough McCarren, L.R. Kelehum, John O'Donnel, Jethro Hampton, Jab. Elliot and George Dean. [13]

Fort Foster proved to be an inviting target once the larger party of soldiers left the area. Leib reports that they were fired upon by a party of Indians. The sentinel in the blockhouse returned fire and the Indians vanished. He reported also that on January 23rd, they were fired upon by a party of at least eight Seminoles, who fired, yelled then disappeared. They heard the same Indians yelling in the forest on the next day.

On 3 February, 1837, a large band of Seminole Indians attacked the fort and attempted to burn down the bridge over the Hillsborough River, hoping to disrupt the supply route from Fort Brooke to Fort King. They had been 'lurking' around the fort for about ten days according to Leib. *"The discharge of one of our field pieces, and a volley of musketry, put them to flight...."*[14]. The sailors fought off the attack and sent to Fort Brooke for re-enforcements. The next day a force of 100 Marines from Fort Brooke arrived at Fort Foster, and the attacks on the fort and bridge let up. The Marines and sailors remained there until they were replaced in late March by army troops. On March 21st Jesup ordered Major Zantzinger to relieve Navy Lt. Leib, with the Marines and sailors of the Concord who had been manning Fort Foster.

Author in the Marine Winter Fatigue Uniform of the period

On 6 March, 1837, the Seminole Chiefs agreed to a treaty which meant that they would be relocated to the western territory. They agreed to move their people to Fort Brooke to await relocation. Marine Captain John Harris was detached to carry the treaty to Washington. Captain Harris was awarded brevet rank of major on 27 January 1837, *"for gallantry and good conduct in the war against Florida Indians, particularly in the affair of the Hatchee-Lustee."* Colonel Commandant Archibald Henderson, who commanded the Marine Regiment during the troublesome times with the Indians, stated in a letter to the Secretary of the Navy that *"Captain Harris while in Florida had command of Mounted Marines and did good service in that capacity."*

On April 1st, Jesup along with Henderson's Marines, Tompkins's Artillery and Major Graham's battalion set out for Tampa Bay. They would remain there and continue patrols around the area and provide guards and protection of the fort. On May 13th, Colonel Henderson and the Marines relieved the Naval Garrison at Fort Brooke completely. Slowly the Indians came in much to the annoyance of Jesup and the others as it seemed they were purposely delaying their arrival for emigration. Things remained peaceful between the antagonists.

The Seminoles as agreed in their treaty, started to arrive at a camp by Fort Brooke, to await transport to the west. Henderson recorded in his journal,

"Camp Hillsborough 7 miles from Tampa

13th April 1837

The Indians come in slowly, but such is their characteristic, & I doubt not they will all be in this month or early in the next. We expect the first emigrating party to start the last of this week. So soon as this takes place, I shall ask orders to return to Washington. I did not wish to be premature in this request, & thereby do away any of the character which the Corps or myself has acquired on this service. I am anxious to leave Florida & our connection with the Army, without the shadow of a strain on our escutcheon, & that the Corps shall return to its stations with and untarnished character. It has gone through campaigns in great harmony with all the Corps, of all sort & kinds, with which it has been associated, regulars, volunteers, Indians & all & will almost uninterrupted good feeling towards all. We have some unquiet spirits among ourselves, which I have endeavored to allay, so that no want of harmony should appear to others. Lieut. Col. Freeman &-&- are hard people to get along with. When we are obliged to come in contact with such men, we must take care to be right, & then they are powerless. They may present benefits from coming to us, but they cannot do much harm."[15]

The Indians indeed came in including Chiefs Jumper, Micanopy, Abraham, Alligator and Caocoochee (Wild Cat) and their people. They congregated in camps a few miles from Fort Brooke, there to await transport to the western lands. While in camp they were able to draw supplies and clothing as many had lost everything. Also groups of whites visited the camps, several of whom were looking for slaves to return to their owners. This made the black Seminoles nervous, many of whom left the camps and went into hiding nearby.

General Jesup knew that this could undo the agreements that he made concerning the Negroes being allowed to emigrate with the Seminoles, and had to stop the visits.

By 23 May, 1837 The Second Seminole War appeared to be over. Henderson relinquished command of the Second brigade and with most of his Marines returned to Washington. He left two companies of Marines under the command of Lieutenant Colonel Samuel Miller and Captain William Dulaney. Henderson received the brevet promotion to brigadier general, the first general of the Marines.

Commodore Dallas who had returned to the *Constellation* at Pensacola in preparation for a patrol off the Mexican coast wrote to General Jesup in April 1837. Believing also that the war was over, he congratulated Jesup and requested the return of his sailors and Marines who were garrisoning posts in Florida. His follow-up letter to Jesup on May 27th, 1837 explains the need for his Marines, *"Marines will be of the utmost importance to me in case I should land which at present I think more than probable, and I have great hopes from your letter of the 15th that I shall receive them before I sail."* Dallas was appreciative of the high regard that Jesup had for his Sailors and Marines, *"... and feel not a little flattered by the manner in which you are pleased to speak of the Officers, Seamen and Marines of the Squadron who have had the good fortune to have cooperated with you."*

In June 1837, Osceola and Sam Jones and their warriors quietly intermingled with the Seminoles at Fort Brooke awaiting relocation and encouraged them to resist. The Seminoles left the area and headed south. The war started again.

Later after Miller returned to Washington, Captain Dulaney remained with the last of the Marine contingent numbering four officers and one hundred seventy Marines under General Jesup's command. Lt. John G. Reynolds and others were assigned to assist in the movement of the Seminoles to their new lands in the Arkansas Territory, later to become Oklahoma. Reynolds had been involved with removal of the Creeks from Alabama, and now led some of the Seminole groups; the first group which had been imprisoned in South Carolina to prevent their escape.

In October 1837, Captain Delaney and his Marines were sent to Punta Rosa at Charlotte harbor to establish a post there. Amos Beebe Eaton US Army made mention of this in his journal. *"23 October. Colonel Cummings issued orders directing the Marines in command of Captain Delaney to proceed to Punta Rosa, Charlotte harbor & there establish a military Post. They left in about 3 days after the order was issued."* 16

They also proceeded up the Sanibel River to establish posts of provisions and to block the Seminoles into the swamp areas. Eaton explained this also.

"11th Nov 37 Col. Smith with his Louisiana Volunteers has recd orders to move to Punta Rosa immediately, with one company of Artillery, where Col S. is to assume command of the Marines now there, then proceed up to Sanybal river & establish depots of Provisions & Forage, then with his force to prevent the Indians, supposed to be about Peace Creek, from retreating to the everglades until the Army from this post can come up on this side. This plan it is supposed will shut them up in a large Cypress Swamp lying south east of Pease Creek, from which retreat they are to be ferreted out—time will show the event." 17

Eaton listed the strength of the forces at that time, and showed the Marine strength at 150. He went on to describe their further movement,

"Dec. 11ᵗʰ '37. The Marines about 110 strong, under the command of Capt. Delany, left for the upper post on the Sanibal this morning in the S.B. Florence."

1838

"The Major General Commanding takes this occasion to express to Captain Dulany and the officers and Marines compassing his command the high sense which he entertains of them good conduct, and of the faithfulness and energy with which they have performed their laborious and often disagreeable duties during the three campaigns they have served under his orders.- He tenders them the thanks of the country, and wishes them success and fame on the new theatre to which they are now called."- General Jesup in regards to the Marines

27 January 1838 this article appeared in the Army Navy Chronicle

Pensacola, Jan 27—The U.S. schr. Grampus sailed hence on yesterday. We understand her destination is St. Marks. Lieut. Waldron commanding the Marines of the West India Squadron goes in her with from 30 to 70 Marines. This force will probably be employed, if necessary in the defense of the frontier settlements, which have been lately assailed by the Indians. We may safely congratulate our fellow citizens upon the efficient protection which the command of Lieut. W. small as it is will be sure to afford. Their commander and the most of them, have already "done the state some service' in this unhappy war.—Gazette.

Extract of a letter, dated TALLAHASSEE, *Florida Feb. 14, 1838.*

"We have been troubled by the Indians in this vicinity; a few buildings have been destroyed, and fears were entertained that they would commit more depredations; but the efficient force of marines, under Lieut. Waldron, so promptly ordered into the interior by Commodore Dallas, has relieved us from all fear and anxiety on this subject. '

"It is reported that an attack has been made on the house of a Mr. Johnson, 20 miles east of this, and Lieut. Waldron has gone in pursuit with the force under his command."

The Squadron Marines continued to be called upon to make forays inland to ward off attacks and hunt down any Seminoles within a short distance from the shore or up the rivers along the coast. These actions were more likened to small boat landing parties than what later became known as 'Riverine Warfare' perfected south in the Everglades.

The following entries are from Jesup's 1838 diary noting some of the movements of the Marines that were left to him from Henderson's regiment during that time. They worked the area from Tampa Bay south along the west coast.

"Jany. 13ᵗʰ. (1838) I went up to Fort Deynaud in the S.B. Phoenix on the 9ᵗʰ, came down to the Bar on the 11ᵗʰ & to Punta Rassa the 112ᵗʰ.

Gen. S. marches on the 11ᵗʰ for Fort Bassinger with the Marines 1 company Arty. & 7 comps Vols

24ᵗʰ March. The Marines serving in the Sanybal District under Capt. Delany came down today. The 2ⁿᵈ Infty has come into Fort Deynaud.

April 20ᵗʰ. Weighed today 157 pounds. The two days past have been windy & very disagreeable. Genl. Jesup has by this established his Hdd Qtrs at Tampa. The 2ⁿᵈ Infty & Marine Corps are yet ignorant of their destination."[18]

As hostilities again seemed to be winding down with more of the Seminoles surrendering for relocation, Jesup started sending some of the units under his command to other locations, including the Marines. Some had already been assigned as was Lt. Reynolds to oversee the relocation of the Seminoles. In his final order to the Marines, he expressed his gratitude for their faithful service under his command.

Order of General Thomas S. Jesup Commanding the Army of the South 30 April, 1838

....

Par: 7 Lt. Terrett of the Marines will repair to New Orleans and relieve Lt. Wharton, 5ᵗʰ infantry in the command of the detachment of recruits now forming a part of the guard to the Indian prisoners at New Orleans.

Par: 8 The detachment of recruits named in paragraph 7, will form under the command of Leiut. Terrett the guard to the Indian prisoners about to leave New Orleans for Arkansas under the charge of Leiut. Reynolds of the Indian Department and will proceed as far as Fort Gibson, from whence it will return to New Orleans under the command of Leiut. Reynolds, and Leiut. Terrett will join from Fort Gibson the command of Captain Dulany in the Cherokee Nation.- On his return to New Orleans Leiut. Reynolds will send the guard to this place subject to the orders of Brigadier General Taylor.--

Par: 9 Leiut. Wharton on being relieved as directed in paragraph 7 will join Captain Hoffman's company of the 6ᵗʰ Infantry now at New Orleans and accompany it to this place.

Par: 10 Captain Dulany will proceed with the Marines under his command to Baton Rouge where he will receive orders in relation to his march to the Cherokee Country.-

The Major General Commanding takes this occasion to express to Captain Dulany and the officers and Marines compassing his command the high sense which he entertains of them good conduct, and of the faithfulness and energy with which they have performed their laborious and often disagreeable duties during the three campaigns they have served under his orders.- He tenders them the thanks of the country, and wishes them success and fame on the new theatre to which they are now called.-

Par: 11 The proper officers of the staff will provide what so ever may be necessary to carry this order into effect.-

By the order of Major General Jesup

E F Chambers

Headquarters, Army of the South

Tampa Bay April 30ᵗʰ, 1838[19]

Although they were ordered north to Baton Rouge to participate in the Cherokee round up, it appears that they either did not participate and were released from the duty, or only spent a month or two as they were welcomed back from their duty in the Indian wars by Commandant Henderson in this address to his returning troops in July of 1838:

"Orders

24th July 1838."

In relation to the return

Of the Battalion of Marines

From Florida

Soldiers,

Two years ago, you left your stations as volunteers for a Single Campaign against the Creek Indians in Alabama. In less than three months after you took your first position in the hostile country on the west bank of the Chattahoochee, you saw the principal Chief of that formidable tribe followed by his whole nation take up his line of march from the banks of the Tallapoosa for his home beyond the Mississippi.

The manner in which you performed your duty there, was such as to elicit an order from the President for a more arduous and hazardous service in the Swamps of Florida.

On the eve of your return to your Stations, this order was received, and your Commandant cannot soon forget how cheerfully you met it. He was your commander in your first Campaign against the Seminoles in their unexplored morasses and his espirit de corps was most amply gratified in the universal tribute paid to your fidelity, exact discipline and untiring perseverance in this arduous and harassing (exhausting) service.

He left you when it was ended and under a belief that your toils were drawing to a close. You were called however to further dangers and exposures and the General with whom you served has borne ample testimony to your conduct during the succeeding Campaign.-

Soldiers-accept the congratulations of your Colonel on your return from a tour of duty equally honorable to yourselves, and to the Corps to which you belong.

Capt. Dulany is relieved from the Command of the Battalion. To him and to its other officers the thanks of their chief are most cordially conveyed. He sincerely wishes they may find an ample reward for all their toils and privations in a return to their homes, and in the assurance that they have elevated their Ancient Corps in the estimation of the Country.-

Arch Henderson
Col. Commandant

Head Quarters of the M. Corps

Washington, 24th July, 1838"

Jesup too was soon to leave Florida not long after Dulaney took the remaining Marines north as he relinquished command.

Even though these were the last of the Marine Regiment that came south with Commandant Henderson, Marines of the West Indies Squadron still assisted with the war effort. Some of these maintained a presence at Fort Dallas (modern day Miami), Fort Lauderdale and Fort Kemble, and with Navy Lieutenant McLaughlin's Mosquito Fleet of canoes and small boats patrolling the Everglades, rivers and inlets in search of the remnants of the Seminole tribes. McLaughlin's force consisted of 160 sailors and Marines, and answered directly to Army General Zachery Scott. The General asked for more men, for McLaughlin and was granted two more companies of Marines.

Seminole bands kept raiding areas around south Florida which kept the naval patrols busy. During 1837-1839, Marines and sailors patrolled the coast of southern Florida, assisting army operations and convoying supplies for them.

Everglades Riverine Warfare

"On the 11th of April, we returned to Key Biscayne, having been living in our canoes for fifty-eight days, with less rest, fewer luxuries, and harder work than fall to the lot of that estimable class of citizens who dig our canals….." Navy Lt. John Rogers describing his expedition through the Everglades.

1839-1842

Marines and Sailors in the Everglades (from the Marine History Center)

By 1839, up to three-fourths of the Seminoles had been removed from Florida. Most of the remaining bands had retreated south of Lake Okeechobee and into the Everglades. The army could not fight this foe using normal means since this was a vast 'sea of grass', and swamps interspersed with areas large enough for the Indians to plant fields of crops and erect small villages deep within this seemingly inhospitable land.

The Navy was constructed for and trained for ship to ship actions and had not been involved in many actions that took them far inshore. During the first few years of the war, the men of the West Indies Squadron received their first experience of what was to become later as 'Riverine Warfare'. They were assigned the task of patrolling the coast of Florida especially the west coast of Florida concentrating on the area from the Withlacoochee River south to Charlotte's Harbor.

They made forays into the Withlacoochee, Homosassa, Crystal and other small rivers along the coast. They also participated in one that involved a long march into the interior along the Myakka River with the army.

29 July 1839 at Key Biscayne, Lt. Mayo had on board his ship, Chief Mad Tiger and his party. When an army boat pulled up alongside, Mad Tiger and his party jumped ship and escaped in their boat. Mayo ordered a pursuit, and in his gig, with the ship's cutter accompanying him, pulled long and hard to catch up with the escaping Indians. Along the way, they were joined by the canoe patrols of Navy Lt. Davis, and Marine Lt. Sloan. After a long pursuit, wherein Mayo was impressed with Mad Tiger's ability to use sail and paddle, the Indians were captured.

12 October, 1839, Captain Mayo landed a party led by Navy Lt. Smith along with 22 sailors and 8 Marines to establish another fort along the Miami River and called this one Fort Dallas as the army had taken over the first one and renamed it.

At Cape Sable, 24 Marines and sailors from the vessel *Ostego* fought off 80 Seminoles on 10 April 1840. Marines garrisoned Fort Kemble near Fort Dallas where Miami is now located. They had built it as a temporary post to protect wood-cutting parties on the Miami River. The Seminoles were very sophisticated fighters. In their raid on Indian Key 130 Seminoles led by Chakaika, (August 6, 1840) made the only amphibious assault ever done by Indians. They plundered the small settlement on Indian Key, killed and mutilated the settlers that they found. Jacob Houseman managed to escape to Tea Table Key where the Navy and Marines had built a small fort, called Fort Spaulding and a small hospital.

There were only a few men there at the time in the hospital as the able bodied men were on patrol. Housman joined Midshipman Francis Key Murray, who with only five fit men and seven of the sick men set sail in their barge for Indian Key. They armed the barge with two small four-pounder cannons, and mistakenly grabbed charges for their six-pounder. As they neared the island, the Indians opened fire on them wounding one man. The Marines and sailors fired their small cannons, and due to the extra-large charges, recoiled over the side of the barge and were not found for thirty-five years.

Another first for this band of Indians, they manned a six-pounder cannon against the rescuers before leaving the island with their plunder. Reinforcements arrived on the 11th under the command of Lt. Rogers from Cape Romano along with his Marines. They had to row almost continuously for twenty-four hours to reach Indian Key.

The next major action the Marines were involved in started in the night of December 31, 1840. Colonel Harney, U.S.Army with Lt. McLaughlin of the Navy with ninety sailors and 60 Marines, twenty dragoons, and seventy soldiers set out from Fort Dallas. They were in five-man and ten-man canoes, keeping in single file and in silence. The men had twenty days rations and sixty rounds of ammunition each. Harney wanted to attack Sam Jones' village. McLaughlin decided that he and his men would continue across the Everglades, once the Colonel achieved his objective and returned to Fort Dallas.

After three nights, they reached Chitto Tustenuggee's old village halfway between Little and New Rivers, where they established a base. They proceeded to their objective and sent in scouts when they closed in on it. The scouts reported back that the camp was deserted. The force spent the a few days scouting the immediate area in search of the Seminoles who had abandoned the village before their arrival.

McLaughlin's group encountered Indians in four canoes, and spread his force out to attack them. In a brief fire fight, three Indians were killed and one wounded, with one of his own men being wounded. The rest of the force responded and they rounded up five of the warriors who escaped the attack.

That evening, Lt. Sloan's Marines and Lt. Edward Ord with his troops of the army cut a trail and after following it for five miles, captured warrior Chia's wife. They responded to noise a little further and Marine Private William Smith was shot in the side when he jumped out of his canoe in pursuit of the warrior who was hidden near where his wife was captured. Chia ran off, reloading his gun while being run down by Sgt. William Searles of the 3rd Artillery. Chia shot him; however Searles managed to grab hold of the warrior and hold him until others caught up to them.

They took the warrior into custody, arriving in time to prevent him from stabbing Searle. After all of this, Chia later agreed to scout for the Mosquito Fleet. He admitted that they had been trying to join Sam Jones' warriors north of New River to continue attacking the American forces.

The joint force returned to Fort Lauderdale to rest, lock up their prisoners and tend to the wounded. Harney then led the group in search of Sam Jones, however they were unable to find any signs of the warriors. When they returned to the fort, Harney let McLaughlin have three of his guides for his planed foray across the Everglades.

McLaughlin set out with his sailors and Marines on a course that took them to Council Island, Alligator Island and the deserted camp of the Prophet. They encountered a canoe of Indians, killed the warrior when he refused to surrender and captured his wife and two children.

They made their way to Chakaika's abandoned camp then turned south to Harney's River which took them to the Gulf. They were the first white men to ever cross the Everglades, arriving on the west coast on January 19, 1841.

Later that year in another joint effort to try to capture Sam Jones and his band, two hundred sailors and Marines entered the Everglades via the Shark River in October 1841. They rendezvoused with Army Captain Burke at Chakaika's Island fifty miles inland. The sixty-seven soldiers from Fort Dallas and the naval unit made their way to Prophet's Landing on the edge of the Big Cypress Swamp. From there they performed many scouting patrols but found no recent signs of the Seminoles.

McLaughlin headed the group south where they spied a couple of Indians in a canoe. They chased them to a camp that had been abandoned. Although they did not capture the Indians, the force managed to destroy approximately sixty acres of crops, peas, beans, pumpkins, along with the camp, equipment and canoes. McLaughlin's party continued north to the Caloosahatchee River where it met up with the *Flirt* at Punta Russa at the mouth of the Caloosahatchee.

Acting on fresh intelligence, McLaughlin agreed to take his men along with the Army troops back into the Everglades in search of Sam Jones. The Seminole had broken away from the Prophet's band. They proceeded back up the Caloosahatchee and into the north section of the glades. They discovered tracks of several Indians and canoes. He sent his guides to follow the trail and try to convince the Indians to surrender if they caught up to them. The detachment waited several days, however the guides did not return. The men then tried to go along the south end of Lake Okeechobee, however bad weather churned up the lake which caused the swamping of some of their canoes.

McLaughlin had to let the men rest along the shore due to several of them becoming ill. At the end of the expedition, he reported that fifteen men died of sickness and up to eighty of them had been ill. The group headed back into the glades to the Locha Hatchie River and on to Key Biscayne, arriving there on December 23rd, 1841.

On January 13th, 1842, Navy Lt. Marchand led one hundred twenty sailors from the *Van Buren* and *Wave*, along with the Marines to patrol the vicinity of Coconut Island. They were unable to enter the Everglades due to the low level of water. They found nothing on their foray.

The following month, Colonel Worth, who was in charge of the actions in Florida by that time, felt that there were so few Seminoles left that it would be best to leave them where they were and end the costly hostilities. When the War Department turned down his suggestion, he decided to withdraw his troops from the endless searches and concentrate on protecting the settlements instead.

McLaughlin decided to extend his patrols into the interior. Worth left him Fort Dallas at which time, McLaughlin assigned Lt. Sloan and his Marines to man that fort. He then requested Worth to leave supplies for his men at Fort Center on Fish Eating Creek for his operations.

McLaughlin's plan was to send two detachments into the Everglades, one to search through the cypress swamps and in the area around the Locha Hatchie, while the other was to search the big Cypress Swamp and headwaters of the Caloosahatchee River. The two groups would make their sweeps all through February and into March, finally rendezvousing at Lake Okeechobee.

The eastern wing was led by Naval Lt. John Rodgers along with Lt. William Herndon, Passed Midshipman George Preble (who in later years became an admiral and wrote a detailed account of the expedition- *"A Canoe Expedition in the Everglades in 1842")'* and Lt. Robert Taylor of the Marines. This group spent fifty-eight days, February 15th through April 11th, 1842, virtually living in their canoes. These canoes were approximately thirty feet long and four feet wide. They each had a chest in the aft portion of the boat which contained the food and supplies, including the extra cartridges sealed in glass jars to protect them from the moisture. At night the officer in charge slept on the chest to ensure no one stole food. Although they were propelled mostly by paddle most of the way, they were also equipped with push poles and small sails.

Preble records the makeup of the expedition:

"Captain Rodgers commanded the expedition arranged as follows: Staff, Lt. John Rodgers Commanding the Scout; Robert Tansall, 2ⁿᵈ Lt. of the Marines, Adjutant; Negro John, wife and child, and John Tigertail, Indian guide. 3 canoes, 4 sailors, 7 Marines. 1ˢᵗ Division (of the) U. S. Schooner Madison: Lt. Wm. L. Herndon Commanding Passed Midshipman S.C.Barney, Asst. Surgeon A.A.Henderson. 6 canoes, 29 men. 2ⁿᵈ Division (of the) U.S. Brigantine Jefferson: Passed Midshipman George H. Preble Commanding; Midshipman C. Benham. 4 canoes, 18 men. 3ʳᵈ Division, Marines: 2ⁿᵈ Lt. R.D.Taylor Commanding. 3 canoes, 17 men. Recapitulation: 16 canoes, 2 Lieuts. 2 Passed Midshipmen, 1 Midshipman, 1 Asst. Surgeon, 2 Lts. Of Marines, 51 sailors, 24 Marines, 1 Indian, 1 Negro, 1 Squaw, 1 Papoose. Total 87 souls."[20]

Preble records that they stopped several times to hunt fresh game, burn several Seminole camps and crops. The Marines under Lt. Taylor and Lt. Tansall patrolled on their own when the expedition found suitable places to make temporary base camps to patrol from. Although they had no direct contact with Seminoles, they did achieve the destruction of many camps, supplies and crops. Rodger's group did manage to make use of some of the supplies left at old Fort Center, and left a small contingent there to guard it. The expedition returned to Key Biscayne after two months.

Preble made many remarks of the beauty of the territory they explored, making many detailed entries about the fauna and flora. They supplemented their food supplies by gathering eggs from the nests of herons, cranes, turkeys, curlews, plovers, and teals. They also ate of the many birds including the 'Grecian Ladies' otherwise called water turkeys, deer, hogs, terrapins (turtles), alligators, raccoons, and on more than one occasion, rattlesnakes and water moccasins. He records that they also ate fish as on more than one occasion, the fish actually jumped into the canoes.

He complained that *"the silence (of the nights) was broken by the screaming of Everglades hens and cranes, the bellowing of frogs and the hooting of owls."* [21]

At some of the small islands they would build small forts of cabbage tree logs, three logs high. From these reinforced base camps, they would send out patrols. Many times the Marines would go by foot instead of canoe when there was enough dry land, or shallow water to allow movement on foot. One such patrol lasted three days of marching through marshes, glades, hammocks and streams.

The expedition explored many streams, creeks and paths as they journeyed up along the Kissimmee River and shores of Lake Okeechobee. They discovered many small villages, some recently abandoned, some, abandoned for several years. They put all of them to the torch as well as the several cultivated fields of corn, water melon, pumpkins and citrus trees.

On March 10th, two sailors deserted never to be heard of again. One of the small islands that they camped on had a large man-made mound. The guides indicated that they could find beads and trinkets in them. Preble offered his men money to dig into it and recover artifacts for him. They found very little. They also camped at the burnt out remains of old abandoned Fort Gardner.

Towards the end of March, Fanny the wife of the Indian guide, Negro John, gave birth to a stillborn child, buried it and continued with her work. On March 31st, they left twelve Marines and eight sailors and two officers at Fort Center to guard their supplies while the rest of the men explored around the area again. The men reached Fort Dulaney on the Okeechobee and camped. The group finally made their way out of the Everglades to Fort Lauderdale and then onto Key Biscayne.

Lt. John Rodgers summed up their conditions in his report, *"On the 11th of April, we returned to Key Biscayne, having been living in our canoes for fifty-eight days, with less rest, fewer luxuries, and harder work than fall to the lot of that estimable class of citizens who dig our canals…"*[22]

Lt. Marchand in charge of the other wing swept the southwest edge of the Everglades, searching the many small keys before entering the glades at Harney's River. They did manage to destroy a cache of supplies the Seminoles had hidden on one of the keys. When they entered the Harney River they did not quite make it to Coconut Island as the water was too low to push on with the canoes.

Marchand made a base camp there and sent out small patrols from there. The Marines and sailors of the expedition cut across trails and on one occasion spotted an Indian or two at a distance, however they always managed to escape.

He moved his force east, following Indian signs and decided not to go to Okeechobee. Instead his force reached the old abandoned Fort Henry, halfway between Fort Dallas and Coconut Island. From there through the rest of March, he sent out patrols. Here again they destroyed vast amounts of crops and whatever small camps and supplies that they found.

The duty in low water of the swamps took its toll on the men. Marchand returned to the coast with his men and returned to Key Biscayne along the coast which was less strenuous on his men. They reached Fort Dallas after forty days of constant duty.

Through April, McLaughlin kept his men on patrols. Lt. Sloan and his Marines conducted sweeps from Fort Dallas among the coontie growing areas in the New River and Miami River area. His unit had some success as by the end of May they had destroyed five small villages. The Seminoles stayed beyond their reach as they alerted all within the area of the troop movements through the use of signal fires.

Second Lt. Taylor and his Marines operated out of Fort Dallas in conjunction with Lt. Marchand and Lt. Rodgers to the west. The groups had such a hard time moving through the area with their canoes and boats due to the low water conditions, that they had to muscle them through the mud in many areas. The going was so tough on the men that Marine Private Jeremiah Kingsbury literally dropped dead in his tracks.

By the end of May, the War Department finally agreed with the many requests of Colonel Worth and determined that all the effort to find and capture the last few hundred Seminoles was not worth the cost in men, materials and money and ordered an end to the war. Thus ended the longest and most expensive of the Indian wars this nation has fought. It also ended the need of Riverine Warfare as developed by Powell and McLaughlin. It gave the Navy and Marines a lasting legacy of extending naval power far inland. In later years it served as the basis of Riverine Warfare in the Civil War and Vietnam War.

Chapter 5

Indian Removal

"With nothing more than a cotton garment thrown over them, their feet bare, they were compelled to encounter cold sleeting storms and to travel over hard frozen ground ...." Lt. J. T. Sprague, April 1, 1837

Marine officers were assigned to overseeing the gathering in camps and in the movement of the Creek Indians from Alabama to their new lands in far off Arkansas Territory, which would later become Oklahoma. Fort Gibson was their destination, and from there they spread out around the surrounding countryside on their new homesteads. These officers took their duty very seriously in protecting the Indians in their charge. Later they would also take charge of the Seminoles from Florida. These are the stories of a few of those officers.

Lt. John T. Sprague, USMC, was in charge of the fifth group of Indians to be sent west. This contingent numbered 1,984 men women and children of all ages. These Creeks came from Kasihta and Coweta towns. He had arrived there on 10 August, 1836 and consulted with Chief Tuck-e-batch-e-hadjo to prepare his people for emigration. After much bantering back and forth about how the people had to bring in their crops, sell their cattle, he made them understand, that they would have to leave when he directed them to do so.

Even so they were not able to leave until 5 September. The contingent was provided for by a government contractor company known as the Alabama Emigrating Company who was responsible for providing wagons and supplies for the journey. Prior to leaving, Sprague had communication with a band of Indians who had been secreted in a nearby swamp throughout the hostilities and were apprehensive of joining in the emigration. He sent word for them to join them without fear of any retribution. They did not join with the main group until the night of the ninth day of their journey. This added another approximately one hundred to one hundred and fifty to the group.

The party now consisted of forty-five wagons, five hundred horses, a large herd of cattle and over two thousand Indians. Along the first part off the journey going through the populated counties, they experienced trouble from people along the way selling them whiskey, and stealing horses, often resulting in violent situations.

The night of the 24th of September after twenty days march, Sprague ordered the contractors to let the party rest for a full day, to which they objected. He related how they argued that at their cost of six to seven hundred dollars a day, it would reduce their profit too much. Sprague insisted that they would abide by their contract which included his authority over them and the condition that *"they should treat the Indians with humanity and forbearance".* The contractors consented. Up to that time, the party had been traveling an average of twelve miles a day. And for the next couple of weeks they had to make at least twenty miles a day due to the lack of water sources. During this stretch of the journey, the contractors again gave Sprague a difficult time about picking up the lame and infirm stragglers, many of whom could not make it to their nightly camp until well after dark.

Sprague covered their contract with them again, showing them that the officer in charge was able to make expenditures necessary, allowing for hiring more wagons. Sprague also indicates in his account of this journey that at no time were the proper rations not issued however there was much inconvenience from not having proper depots of provisions along the way. The Indians had to gather corn along the way to supplement their rations which delayed them from making their meals some days until well after dark.

One of the problems with the stragglers was due to groups obtaining liquor along the way and as he wrote, "*the men and women would congregate there, and indulge in the most brutal scenes of intoxication. If any white-man broke in upon these bacchanals he did it at the imminent hazard of his life*". [2]These groups caused problems with the sober Indians as well as any whites around the encampments.

They arrived at Memphis, Tennessee on the 9th of October and remained there until the 27th. There he met with the president of the contractors and made his complaints known. Mr. Gibson was made aware of the full content of his contracts, and replaced one of his agents for the remainder of the journey.

There were now assembled outside Memphis, thirteen thousand Indians as the previous groups had encamped there until all groups had arrived. On the eleventh, their steam boats arrived to start ferrying the groups across the Mississippi. The nervous citizenry of the area was relieved when the city council banned the sale of any liquor to Indians, thus helping to assure tranquility during their stay.

After a brief rest the five groups were headed out. From Memphis, most of them would descend the Mississippi to the White River and seventy miles up that river avoiding the swampy Mississippi lands. Sprague conferred with the chiefs, contractors and other officers, and decided to take his group down the Mississippi to the Arkansas River then up to Little Rock. By taking this route, his group shaved a trek by foot of one hundred and fifty miles.

Approximately seven hundred of the Indian men and some of the contractors took the horse heard through the swampy area, while their women, children and older people went by steam boat with two large flat boats towed behind. They left on the journey October 27th and arrived at Little Rock on November 3rd. They had the advantage of having full rations ahead of the other four groups.

The Arkansas River was flowing fast, so the Indians on board the steam boat had to be separated into two groups so that the boat could safely navigate the currents. The Indians who had taken the horses on the land route, caught up with them on the 4th.

Due to the abundant supply of whiskey at Little Rock, Sprague decided to move the group to Potts, Arkansas where the five groups were supposed to gather. He sent the steam boat back to gather stragglers. A large group of the Indians who had taken the horses through the swamp had remained behind to hunt, and refused to leave there. Even his assistant Agent Mr. Freeman and others were unable to convince the group to leave the swamp.

Once the steam boat reached Sprague and the main group, he placed all the sick and older Indians on it along with Doctor Hill, and sent them on to Fort Gibson, where they arrived on November 22nd.

The agents who had retuned unsuccessfully from the swamp reached the encampment on the 17th, and Sprague decided not to delay the movement any longer. The weather was getting colder, and many of the Indians were not properly clothed for the change in temperatures.

"The sufferings of the Indians at this period were intense. With nothing more than a cotton garment thrown over them, their feet bare, they were compelled to encounter cold, sleeting storms and to travel over hard frozen ground. Frequent appeals were made to me to clothe their nakedness and to protect their lacerated feet. To these I could do no more than what came within the provisions of the Contract. I ordered the party to halt on the 22nd and proceeded again on the 23rd. The weather was still severe, but delay only made our condition worse. The steam boat, on its return from Fort Gibson, fortunately found us encamped near the river Spadra. On board of her I succeeded in getting nearly the whole party now to some sixteen hundred souls. The boat started again for Fort Gibson on the 24th. Those that determined to go by land were all mounted or in wagons and I directed them to proceed as fast as possible. On the 30th we learned that owing to the rapid fall of the Arkansas, the boat had grounded. We soon came in the vicinity of her; wagons were procured and this body from the boat soon joined those on shore. The Indians here were frequently intoxicated. They procured liquor from other Indian residents of the country and the artifices of both combined no man could detect. On the 7th of December, when within eighteen miles of Fort Gibson, I again halted the party, and agents were sent back to bring up all that could be

found in the rear. This being done, we started the following morning, and arrived at Fort Gibson on the 19ᵗʰ inst. By order of Brigadier General Arbuckle, I encamped the party in the vicinity of the fort."[3]

Once the agents returned with all who had straggled behind, Sprague got a total head count and listed 2,237. This was 150 more than he had originally started with, which accounts for the group who had joined them on the march. Once blankets and other items were disbursed to the Indians, Sprague marched them thirty five miles beyond the fort where they were to pick out their land for settlement on the 20th.

He calculated that since leaving Chambers County Alabama, they spent ninety-six days traveled eight hundred miles on land and four hundred and twenty-five by water. His accounts record twenty-nine deaths, fourteen of whom were children, the rest *"aged, feeble and intemperate"*..

Sprague summed up his experience with the Creeks on this long journey thus;

"So long a journey under the most favorable auspices must necessarily be attended with suffering and fatigue. They were in a deplorable condition when they left their homes, and a journey of upwards of a thousand miles could not certainly have improved it. There was nothing within the provisions of the contract by which the Alabama Emigrating Company could contribute to their wants, other than the furnishing of rations and transportation, and a strict compliance with the demands off the officer of the government; these demands, unquestionably, must come within the letter and spirit of the contract. All these they complied with. The situation of the officers of the Government, at the head of these parties, was peculiarly responsible and embarrassing. They were there to protect the rights of the Indians and to secure to them all the Government designed for them. These Indians, looking up to the officers as a part of the Government, not only appealed for their rights, but their wants. They could sympathize with them, as everyone must who saw their condition, but could not relieve them. They had nothing, within their power, for in a pecuniary point they were scarcely better off than those they were willing to assist. All

that the contract granted was secured to them. But all this could not shield them from the severity of the weather, cold sleeting storms, and hard frozen ground.

   Had a few thousand dollars been placed at the disposal of the officer which he could have expended at his discretion, the great sufferings with all ages, particularly the young, were subjected to, might have been in a measure avoided. But as it was, the officer was obliged to listen to their complaints without any means of redress"......

"Had they been permitted to retain the fair proceeds of their lands they would have had the means of procuring any additional supplies for their comfort. The stipulations of the treaty were fairly executed; all that was to be furnished to the Indians was provided, and if they were inadequate to their comfortable removal and subsistence, no blame can be attached to the agents of the Alabama Emigrating Company or to the officers of the government."[4]

His frustration with the conditions of the assignment and sufferings of his charges is evident in his writings.

A few of the members of the Kasihta Town Creeks drew up a letter concerning their experience; *"You have been with us many moons, you have heard the cries of our women and children our road has been a long one and on it we have laid the bones of our men, women, and children. When we left our homes the great General Jesup told us that we could get to our country as we wanted to. We wanted to gather our crops, and we wanted to go in peace and friendship. Did we? No! We were drove off like wolves, lost our crops, and our peoples' feet were bleeding with long marches. Tell General Jackson if the white man will let us we will live in peace and friendship, but tell these agents (emigrating contractors) came not to treat us well, but make money and tell our people behind not to be drove off like dogs. We are men... we have women and children, and why should we come like wild horses?"*

Even still they did appreciate Sprague's efforts on their part.

Sprague reported the successful completion of his mission in his letter to the Commissioner of Indian Affairs:

Fort Gibson, Aks.
December 20th 1836

Sir

I have the honour of informing you, that the whole number of the 5th detachment of emigrating Creek Indians in my charge, amounting to two thousand and eighty seven, are here, and received by Capt. Stephenson U.S. Army and are encamped within a mile of the Fort by order of General Arbuckle.

When my last communication to the Department of the 21st of October was written, arrangements were made at Memphis for all the Indians to be landed at Rock Rowe [halfway between Arkansas Post and Little Rock] immediately, west of the Mississippi swamp. Two parties were to precede mine and I saw that our detention would be longer than could be desired. The Indians being very impatient, the Agents of the Company accepted my proposal to take the Party to Little Rock by water, as all reports respecting the stage of the Arkansas River were favorable. I consulted the chiefs who readily acquiesced. A good sized steam boat [the "John Nelson"] was procured, and this, with two large flats, were found sufficient to contain all that were not going through the swamp, which were mostly women and children. On the 26th of October about six hundred men and women with all the ponies belonging, to the Party, started for the swamp in charge of my assistant Mr. Freeman. The Agents of the Company assured me that abundant provisions were made for them on the route, which proved to be the case. On the following morning, the 27th the party in my immediate charge left Memphis, having on board all the boats, as near as could be estimated, fifteen hundred souls. When we arrived at the mouth of the Arkansas the waters being so high and the current so strong, it was impossible to proceed with both flatboats in tow, and the only alternative was, to leave one and go up as fast as possible with the other. Every provision was made for the wants and comfort of the Indians that remained.

The 3rd of November we arrived at Little Rock and the next day the boat returned and brought up those left behind. The Indians that came through the swamp joined us sixty miles from Little Rock. I halted the party at the Dandanelles, a point on the Arkansas River to give all an opportunity to get up with us, while there, one of the companies steam boats belonging to the Company came up bound to Fort Gibson, on board of which, I succeeded in getting the lame, sick, and aged, and so many more of the party as were disposed to go. This detachment, amounting to three hundred and ninety five arrived in their new country twelve miles from Fort Gibson, on the 21st Ultimo, where they were received by Capt. Stephenson.

This boat on its return met us again near the river Spadra. I urged the Indians to go on board as the severity of the weather and the bad state of the roads would make them suffer severely. About twelve hundred consented and the remainder continued on by land. When we arrived opposite Fort Smith we learnt that the boat had grounded owing to the rapid fall of the river and that the Indians were on shore. Waggoners were immediately procured and the party were soon together and on the way to Fort Gibson, which we soon reached after a fatiguing journey of ninety five days from Chambers county, Alabama.

The health of the Party has been very good, and the feeling, on the part of the Indians is of the most friendly character. On our own arrival here, Genl. Arbuckle, deeming it necessary that a perfect understanding should exist between the Indians and the hostiles who were emigrated last summer, ordered the Party to halt until everything could be amicably arranged. This has been done, and as soon as they received their blankets they start for their new homes. In my letter to the Department of the 21st of October I expressed my dissatisfaction of the course pursued by the Agents of the Alabama Company. The duties of the officer in charge being so much at variance with the interests of the company differences of opinion will unavoidably occur. It, however, now affords me pleasure to say, that, they have adopted every measure which I deemed expedient, and done all in their power to contribute to the comfort and convenience of the Indians. A stupid indifference to the stipulations of the contract, and a disposition to break down the authority of the officer, and drive the Indians far beyond their powers, seemed to be the determination of these Agents; but though this did exist, I cannot now, in justice, withhold from them my arrival, that they have complied with the contract and endeavored to act up to its letter and spirit.

I am, with great respect
You obt servant
J. T. Sprauge
Lt & Milty Agt 5th Detachment Emgt C. Indian

To
C. A. Harris Esqr.
Commissioner of Indian Affairs
*War Department, Washington, D.C.*₅

He later described in great detail the hardships encountered on the way:

Washington City, April 1, 1837

Sir

On the 3rd of August 1836, in compliance with an order from Major General Jesup, commanding the Army of the South, I reported to him in person for emigrating duty. After being engaged in the various duties connected with the large bodies of Indians in the vicinity of Tuskegee, Al. from the 3d to the 8th inst. I received a verbal order from him to report forthwith to the Cuseter and Coweta towns of Indians, and prepare them for immediate removal

On my arrival at these towns on the 10th, I had an interview with the principal chief, Tuck-e-batch-e-hadjo, and urged upon him the necessity of taking immediate measures to prepare his people for emigration. To this, after raising every argument against it, he reluctantly consented. His principal reasons were, that his peoples crops were not gathered - their cattle were not sold, and that the time specified for their departure was earlier than he anticipated.

The following day, I assembled all the chiefs, and explained to them that the necessary arrangement to embody their towns, in order to transfer them to the charge of the Alabama Emigrating Company upon such a day as might be designated by the Commanding General. They gave no other than a silent acquiescence to my wishes, but expressed among themselves strong feelings of dissatisfaction. I promised them every assistance in disposing of what little they had, but assured them that upon the day fixed for their departure they must be ready. The necessity of their leaving their country immediately was evident to every one; although wretchedly poor they were growing more so every day they remained. A large number of the white-men were prowling about, robbing them of their horses and cattle and carrying among them liquors which kept up an alarming state of intoxication. The citizens of the country had no security, for though these Indians had professed the most friendly feelings, no confidence could be placed in them, as the best informed inhabitants of the country believed them to be allied with those who had already committed overt acts of hostility. Some families which has fled for safety were afraid to return until the country was rid of every Indian. Public indignation was strong against them, and no doubt the most serious consequences would have resulted, had not immediate measures been adopted for their removal. In this state of things, however indignant their feelings or however great the sacrifice, it was but justice to get them out of the country as soon as possible.

On the 23d inst. I received orders from the commanding General to move the Party on the 29 inst. The time, however, was prolonged five days, to the 3d of September. On the 1st of September I had in camp near two thousand ready for removal. This number comprised the whole of the two towns, excepting a few who had been secreted in a swamp from the commencement of the Creek War. These sent an express to know if I would receive them as friends should they come in. I assured them they would be treated like the rest. I heard no more from them until the ninth night of our march, when, they joined the train with their woman and children. Their number I could never learn, as they kept themselves aloof lest they might be treated as hostiles; but from other Indians, who were very silent on the subject, I learnt there were from one hundred to one hundred and fifty. The 3d of September I placed all the Indians under my charge in care of Mr. Felix G. Gibson and Charles Abercrombie, members of the Alabama Emigrating Company, and on the morning of the 5th the Party started for Arkansas, arranged to wagons according to the contract. The train consisted of forty-five wagons of every description, five hundred ponies and two thousand Indians. The moving of so large a body necessarily required some days to effect an arrangement to meet the comfort and convenience of all.

The marches for the first four or five days were long and tedious and attended with many embarrassing circumstances. Men, who had never had claims upon these distressed beings, now prayed upon them without mercy. Fraudulent demands were presented and unless some friend was near, they were robbed of their horses and even clothing. Violence was often resorted to to keep off these depredators to such an extent, that unless forced marches had been made to get out of this and the adjoining counties the Indians would have been wrought to such a state of desperation that no persuasion could have deterred them from wreaking their vengeance upon the innocent as well as the guilty.

As soon as time and circumstances would permit, proper arrangements were made to secure to the Indians, regularly, their rations and transportation. A large herd of cattle were driven ahead of the train which supplied the Party with fresh beef. Two days rations were issued every other day, while corn was issued every day. The Party moved on without any serious inconvenience other than the bad state of the roads and frequent drunken [brawls], until the 22, when from the warmth of the weather and the wearied condition of the Indians, I deemed it expedient to halt for a days rest. Tuck-e-batch-e-hadjo, the principal chief, had been desirous of stopping sooner, and had exposed his determination to do so. The situation of the Camp at the time was not a desirable one for a halt, nor was I inclined to indulge him. I ordered the train to proceed, he with reluctance came on. From the first days march, I saw a disposition in the Indians, among both young and old, to remain behind. From their natural indolence and for their utter disregard for the future, they would straggle in the rear dependant upon what they could beg, steal or find, for support. I used every entreaty to induce them to keep up, but finding this of no avail I threatened them with soldiers and confinement in irons. This had a salutary effect, and was the means of bringing most of them into Camp in good season. On the night of the 24th inst. the Party encamped at Town Creek, Al., after twenty days march averaging about twelve miles a day. I waited on the contractors and requested them to halt the Party the following day. To this they expressed their unqualified disapprobation and denied my authority to exercise such a power. Their expenses they said were from six to seven hundred dollars per day, and if such authority was given or implied in the contract their hopes of making any thing were gone. I assured them, that from the condition of the Indians, the common calls of humanity required it, and that one of the stipulations of the contract was, that they should treat the Indians with humanity and forbearance. I ordered the Indians to halt, and told the Contractors they could act their own pleasure; either go on with their empty wagon or remain. The Party halted and resumed the journey on the following morning, the 26th. The Indians and horses were evidently much relieved by this days rest. From this period to the fifth of October our marches were long, owing to the great scarcity of water; no one time, however, exceeding twenty miles. The Indians in large numbers straggled behind and many could not get to Camp till after dark.

These marches would not have been so burdensome had proper attention been paid to the starting of the Party in the morning. It was necessary that their baggage as well as their children should be put in the wagons, and the sick and feeble sought out in the different parts of the Camp. But this was totally disregarded. I reminded the Contractors that the party now required the utmost attention, that unless they were strictly seen to, we should not at night have more than half the Indians in Camp. To this they were indifferent, saying, that they must keep up or be left. Early in the morning the waggons moved off, the Agents at the head, leaving those behind to take care of themselves. It's an absurdity to say, that Indians must take care of themselves; they are men it is true, but it is well known that they are totally incapable of it, and it's proverbial that they will never aid each other. To this course of proceeding I remonstrated, and the tenth article of the contract which authorizes the officers to make any expenditures contributing to the comfort and convenience &c.,. I put in execution, which relieved the Indians from the destitute situation in which they otherwise have been placed. My letters to the Contractors accompanying this report embrace this period and will explain to you more fully the course I was compelled to adopt. It, however, affords me pleasure to say, that upon a better knowledge of their obligations, they very readily consented to pay the expenses which accrued in keeping up the rear.

On the 5th of October I again halted the party and rested one day. To this the contractors objected and seemed determined to drive the Indians into their measures. The 7th the Party again moved and on the 9th inst. encamped near Memphis, Tenn. Great inconvenience was experienced upon this entire route for the want of depots of provisions. There was no time when the proper rations were not issued, but from the frequent necessity of gathering and hauling corn, the Indians were often obliged to take their rations after dark. This caused great confusion and many were deprived of their just share. Though the neglect of these Agents in not bringing up the rear of the party deserves the severest reprehension, yet, I must in frankness acknowledge that there were many who not come up under the most favorable circumstances. This, however, was no apology for not bringing up those who would or at least making an effort. If liquor could be found upon the road, or within four or six miles of it, men and women would congregate there, and indulge in the most brutal scenes of intoxication. If any white man broke in upon these bacchanals he did it at the imminant hazard of his life. Often in this state, they would come reeling and singing into camp late at night, threatening the lives of all who came within their reach - alarming the citizens of the country, and not unfrequently creating the most indignant feelings among the sober Indians towards all the white men who were about them. They would taunt them as cowards and dare them to join them in some nefarious act. Without the means of quelling such restless spirits by the strong arm of power, the most kind and conciliatory feelings should have been evinced towards them. But unfortunately for me, these Agent entertained no such sentiments. At Memphis I met a number of contractors and before them I laid my complaints and convinced them, that if no remedy was provided, I was determined to relieve the company of their charge of the Indians, and take the arduous responsibility of taking them to Arkansas myself. The President of the Company in a highly honorable measure declared that nothing should be left undone to meet the wishes of the officers of the Government. These Agents, I either wanted dismissed or taught the first lesson of the obligations they had assumed. One of the Agents left the Party, and it was afterwards in charge of Mr. Gibson and Gilman. Here, I think, for the first time read the contract, and I found in him ever after a willingness to comply with what I considered expedient for the comfort and convenience of the Indians. With such indication of a proper interpretation and understanding of the contract, and upon the assurance of the most respectable men belonging to the company, I could have no hesitation in giving them an opportunity to redeem their pledges.

At Memphis we remained from the 9th of October until the 27th. The Mississippi was here to be crossed, and the Company were much disappointed in not finding their steam boats as they anticipated. The boats, however, arrived on the 11th; Captain Batemans party were the first to cross, Lieutenant Scrivens was the second, and my own the third, Lieutenant Deas and Mr., Campbells parties were in the rear. The assembly of thirteen thousand Indians at one point, necessarily made our movements slow. This detention was of advantage to the Indians as it gave them rest and afforded the sick and feeble an opportunity to recover. The required rations were furnished them regularly within this time, and they all conducted with the greatest propriety. The Common Council of the City passed an ordinance prohibiting the sale of liquor, which added greatly to their comfort, and to the peace and security of the citizens.

The Mississippi Swamp at this season was impassable for wagons, and it was agreed, that the horses should go through while the women and children with their baggage took steam boats to Rock Row. This place was attained by descending the Mississippi about one hundred miles to the mouth of White River, and ascending this river about seventy miles, and thereby avoiding a swamp about fifty miles in breadth.

Finding that the embarkation of the parties that preceded mine would cause much delay, a mutual agreement was effected between the chiefs, the contractors and myself to take the party up the Arkansas River to Little Rock. The advantages to be gained by this were evident; it put us ahead of all the other parties, secured us an abundant supply of provisions, and avoided a tedious journey of one hundred and fifty miles on foot. A commodious steam boat was procured and upon this, and two flat boats, I put as near as could be estimated, fifteen hundred women & children and some men, with their baggage. The men amounting to some six or seven hundred passed through the swamp with their horses, in charge of my assistant Agent Mr. Freeman. I received every assurance, that upon this route, the necessary provision was made for them.

On board the boats, an abundance of corn and bacon were stored for the party to subsist upon until we should reach Little Rock. On the 27th the boat started. The Indians were comfortably accommodated, sheltered from the severity of the weather and from the many sufferings attending a journey on foot. The boats stopped at night for them to cook and sleep, and in the morning resumed the journey. The current of the Arkansas being so strong at this time, it was found expedient to leave a part of the Indians until the boat could go up and return. These were left in the care of an Agent with the necessary supplies. On the 3d of November we arrived at Little Rock. The larger portion of the party which passed through the swamp, joined us the 4th. Many remained behind and sent word, that when they got bear skins enough to cover them they would come on. Here, they felt independent, game was abundant and they were almost out of the reach of the white-men. At first, it was my determination to remain at Little Rock until the whole party should assemble. But from the scarcity of provisions and the sale of liquor, I determined to proceed up the country about fifty miles and there await the arrival of all the Indians.

Tuck-e-batch-e-hadjo refused to go, "we wanted nothing from the white-men and should rest". Every resting place with him, was where he could procure a sufficiency of liquor. The petulant and vindictive feelings which this chief so often evinced, detracted very much from the authority he once exercised over his people. But few were inclined to remain with him.

The 12th we encamped at Potts, the place designated for the concentration of the whole party. My assistant Agent, together with three Agents of the Company, returned immediately to bring up and subsist all in the rear. Some of them went as far back as the Mississippi Swamp. They collected, subsisted and transported all they could get to start by every argument and entreaty. A body of Indians under a secondary chief Narticker-tustunuggee expressed their determination to remain in the swamp in spite of every remonstrance. They evinced the most hostile feelings and cautioned the white-men to keep away from them. The 14th the steam boat that returned from Little Rock to bring up those left on the Arkansas, arrived at our encampment with Tuck-e-batch-e-hadjo and his few adherents on board. On this boat the following day I put all the sick, feeble and aged; placed them in charge of Doctor Hill the surgeon of the party, with instruction to proceed to Fort Gibson, and there be governed by the proper officer at that place. This party arrived at their place of destination on the 22d inst., and were received by the officer of the proper department. The Agents bringing up the rear arrived at Camp on the 17th. Those in the swamp still persisted in their determination to remain. Neither the Agents or myself, had any means by which we could force them into proper measures, most conducive to their comfort and progress. The season being, far advanced and the weather daily becoming, more severe, I ordered the party to proceed the following morning. The sufferings of the Indians at this period were intense. With nothing more than a cotton garment thrown over them, their feet bare, they were compelled to encounter cold sleeting storms and to travel over hard frozen ground. Frequent appeals were made to me to clothe their nakedness and to protect their lacerated feet. To these I could do no more than what came within the provisions of the contract. I ordered the party to halt on the 22d and proceeded again on the 23d. The weather was still severe, but delay only made our condition worse. The steam boat on its return from Fort Gibson, fortunately, found us encamped near the river Spadra. On board of her I succeeded in getting nearly the whole party, amounting now to some sixteen hundred souls. The boat started again for Fort Gibson on the 24th. Those that determined to go up by land were all mounted or in waggons, and I directed them to proceed as fast as possible. On the 30th we learnt, that owing to the rapid fall of the Arkansas the boat had grounded. We soon came in the vicinity of her, waggons were procured and this body from the boat soon joined those on shore. The Indians here were frequently intoxicated. They procured liquor from other Indian residents of the Country, and the artifices of both combined no man could detect. On the 7th of December, when within eighteen miles of Fort Gibson I again halted the party, and agents were sent back to bring up all that could be found in the rear. This being done we started the following morning, and arrived at Fort Gibson on the 10th inst. By the order of Brigadier General Arbuckle I encamped the party in the vicinity of the Fort. Many reports were in circulation that the Creeks settled in the country were inimical to the emigrants, and it was deemed advisable to have a perfect understanding among all parties previous to entering their new country. This was effected to the satisfaction of all, but how long it will last the future can only tell. Two Agents belonging to my party, who had remained behind, arrived on the 15th, bringing on all they could find or gather all that were willing to come, a few they said were behind.

As soon as I was satisfied that all were present that could be brought up, I had the number counted as correctly as circumstances would admit. The number present was twenty two hundred and thirty seven. The number, for which I required of the Company rations and transportation, was two thousand and eighty seven; leaving one hundred and fifty that were not enrolled. This number, no doubt, were the hostiles who joined the train on the march. I could never obtain from the Indians, nor from any one identified with them, any satisfactory information respecting their number or how they subsisted. Their friends, doubtless, shared their rations with them to prevent their being enrolled, lest they might be treated with severity. I gave them every assurance of friendship, but it had no avail. On the 20th inst, the officer of the Government appointed to receive the Emigrating Creeks, acknowledged the receipt of my entire party.

To Captain Stephenson of the Army, who performs this task, I am greatly indebted for the many facilities he granted me in the performance of my duties. He is untiring in the department assigned to him and discharges his obligations with promptness and fidelity.

After the Indians had received their blankets in compliance with the treaty, I preceded with the larger portion of them to their country assigned them. Thirty five miles beyond Fort Gibson I encamped them upon a prairie, and they soon after scattered in every direction, seeking a desirable location for their new homes. The better understanding, of the contract by these Agents, and the establishment of depots of provisions on the route from the Mississippi, contributed greatly to facilitate our progress, and to the "comfort and convenience" of the Indians. The duties of the officers in charge of these parties being so much at variance with the interests of the company, difference of opinion will unavoidably occur. The requirements of the Indian are against the interests of the Company. One party is actuated by interest, the other by humanity. I was there to protect the rights of the Indian; the course was a straight one and I pursued it. But though these misunderstandings did occur, the agents accompany the parties deserve great credit for their perseverance. The ready acquiescence of the Agents of my detachment to all my wishes, after crossing the Mississippi, deserves my decided approbation; they were unremitting in every emergency.

The excessive bad state of the roads, the high waters, and the extreme cold and wet weather, was enough to embarrass the strongest minds. The distance traveled by the Party from Chambers county, Alabama to their last encampment, was eight hundred miles by land, and four hundred & twenty five miles by water; occupying ninety six days. The Health of the Indians upon the entire route was much better than might been anticipated. Twenty nine deaths were all that occurred; fourteen of these were children and the others were the aged, feeble and intemperate. The unfriendly disposition of the Indians towards the whites from the earliest history of our country, is known to everyone. To what an extent this feeling existed in the party under my charge, I cannot with confidence say, for it was seldom expressed but when in a state in intoxication. But if this be a fair criterion, I have no hesitation is saying it was of the most vindictive and malignant kind. To say they were not in a distressed and wretched condition, would be in contradiction to the well known history of the Creeks for the last two years. They were poor, wretchedly, and depravedly poor, many of them without a garment to cover their nakedness. To this there was some exceptions, but this was the condition of a larger portion of them. They left their country at a warm season of the year, thinly clad, and characteristically indifferent to their rapid approach to the rigors of a climate to which they were unaccustomed, they expended what little they had for intoxicating drinks or for some gaudy article of jewelry.

So long a journey, under the most favorable auspices must necessarily be attended with suffering and fatigue. They were in a deplorable condition when they left their homes, and a journey of upwards of a thousand miles could not certainly have improved it. There was nothing within the provisions of the contract by which the Alabama Emigrating Company could contribute to their wants, other than the furnishing of rations and transportation, and a strict compliance with the demands of the officer of the Government; these demands, unquestionably, must come within the letter and spirit of the Contract. All these they complied with. The situation of the Officers of the Government at the head of these parties was peculiarly responsible and embarrassing. They were there to protect the right of the Indians, and to secure to them all the Government designed for them. These Indians looking up to the officers as part of the Government, not only appealed for their rights, but their wants. They could sympathize with them, as everyone must who saw their condition, but could not relieve them. They had nothing within their power, for in a pecuniary point they were scarcely better off than those they were willing to assist. All that the contract granted was secured to them, but all this, could not shield them from the severity of the weather, cold sleeting storms, and hard frozen ground. Had a few thousand dollars been placed at the disposal of the officer which he could have expended at his discretion, the great sufferings which all ages, particularly the young, were subjected to, might have been in a measure avoided. But as it was, the officer was obliged to listen to their complaints without any means of redress. Captain Batemans was the first party to arrive at Fort Gibson, my own was the second, Mr. Campbells the third, Lt. Screvens the fourth and Lt. Deas the fifth. I have conversed with all these gentlemen since the delivery of their parties, excepting Mr. Campbell, and I believe they will concur with me fully in my views and opinions. With all the officers I held almost daily intercourse when upon the road, and I can bear testimony, to the faithful discharge of the arduous duties that devolved upon them. They all complained of the difficulty in making the Indians keep up with the moving train.

The following is an extract of a letter from Lt. Deas who was in the rear, addressed to me when I was waiting the arrival of my party from the rear.

"The Agent of the company, with my party, requests we to write you upon the subject of your Indians that have remained behind your party. He says that he has ample means to bring up all that straggle from whatever party, and it is not my intention to allow any of the emigrating Indians to remain upon the route of emigration if I can possibly prevent it."

I believe every effort was made to keep them up, but nothing but the rigor of military authority can ever effect it. Many exaggerated reports are in circulation repeating the miserable condition of these emigrating Indians. Let these be traced to the proper source, and it will be found that the white-men with whom they have been associated for years past have been the principal cause. There is enough in support of this opinion. It is only necessary to advert to the allegation, in many instances well established, of the lands of the Indians having been purchased by some of these citizens at prices much below their real value, or of the purchase money having been in whole or part, withheld; to the prosecutions for valid or fictitious debts commenced at the moment of their departure for the west, and thereby extorting from them what little money they had.

Had they been permitted to retain the fair proceeds of their lands, they would have had the means of procuring any additional supplies required for their comfort.

The stipulations of the treaty were fairly executed; all that was to be furnished the Indians was provided, and if these were inadequate to their comfortable removal and subsistence, no blame can be attached to the Agents of the Alabama Emigrating Company or to the officers of Government.

I have the honour to be

Very Respectfully

Your Obt Servant

J.T. Sprague

Lt. U.S. M. Corps

& Military Agent

5th Detachment Emigrating Creek[6]

Marine Lt. John G. Reynolds and Lt. Thomas Sloan had been assigned to oversee the encampments of the families of the Creek warriors who had volunteered to go to Florida to fight the Seminoles for General Jesup. These families were allowed to delay their emigration until their husbands returned from their duty in Florida. In December of 1836, a group of hostile Creeks under Chief Tuskeneah near the encampment had attacked the plantation owned by Doctor Battle on Cowagee Creek. A few weeks later they attacked the plantation of Lewis Pugh also along the Cowagee.

Local militia caught up with some of those responsible and killed several of them. However this did not appease the locals. The Creeks serving in Florida were to be released from service in February; however General Jesup persuaded them to stay on a few extra months. The locals were not pleased with the agreement and wanted all Indians out of their locale immediately. This led to those in the encampments being forced out by the Alabama and Georgia militias, against whom, Reynolds and Sloan were powerless to prevent the abuses with the few men that they had. They did manage to keep things from escalating into a more serious tragedy.

Locals petitioned Reynolds to collect the firearms from the Indians in his camp to ensure that they would not join in with the others. Reynolds did so in an effort to keep the peace. However, not satisfied with so many Indians remaining in the area, in February 1837, militia from Russell County Alabama, and Franklin County Georgia entered the encampment after burning the residence and confiscating property and Negroes and young Indian boy of Anne Curnell, a half-breed Indian woman.

A few days later the troops returned and started to take prisoners of the men. Reynolds protested, however the few armed men that he had stood no chance in stopping the raid. General Wellborne of the militia refused to desist his actions and took over two hundred and fifty prisoners. These people had the government's pledge that *'the faith of the government had pledged to the Creek warriors then helping the United States in Florida, that those remaining behind should be wholly unmolested by the citizens, and placed under the protection of the United States.",[7]* insisted Reynolds.

Later that night, shots were heard beyond the camp, and it was learned that a ninety year old Indian, Loche Yahola had been shot as well as a fifteen year old girl who had run from some men who tried to assault her.

To prevent the militia from carrying out their threat of taking the male prisoners to Tuskegee, Reynolds asked the Indians if they would want to leave the area instead of being separated, they agreed to leave. Reynolds organized them, and in thirty-six hours, he had 1,900 of the Indians of his charge, with only five four-horse teams on the move west.

Reynolds reported in his report of March 31, 1837:

Fort Morgan

Mobile Point

31 Mch 1837

Major,

In obedience to your call for information respecting the causes which led to the removal of the families of the Indian Warriors now in Florida, from the Creek Nation, the ___ sustained by them in consequence of such removal. I have to state in answer to the first – that I am entirely ignorant as to any just causes for such a measure – my Indians now perfectly friendly and obedient men ever ready to carry in to effect measures or requirement I might deem necessary to make with the exception of a few residing near to the late Chief Tuskenniahaws residence, and they were not at all times otherwise disposed, but at periods when Tuskenea put forth his influence under the guidance of some few designing white men, I have had trouble. When the settlers became agitated by the depredation committed on the plantation of Doct. Battle on Comega Creek, I deemed it prudent & proper to allay their fears by collecting in the rifles –I appointed a day for that purpose and attended in person for the reception of those, of Jim Boy's & Elk Cahadjo's warriors, all men forthcoming the day subsequent was allotted for the handing in of Todkineas people, from the previous conduct of Tuskemia. I was apprehensive my requirements would not be complied with, in which event Wm. Felton my principal assistant was directed to repair to Tuskegee and report the results. My anticipations being realized, I arrested Tuskemia that night and brought him to Tuskegee where he was detained three days during which period twenty one rifles were handed in & he made perfectly sensible of his situation, he was permitted to return to his house since when I have experienced not the slightest difficulty he has done much towards bringing his people into camp. These facts were duly reported to Capt. Page. The emigrating Creek agent and commanding officer of the nation.

On the evening of 9th February after the warriors of Lt. Sloan's camp had been placed in the pickets at Tuskegee, a company under Capt. Howard returning by the Old Federal Road halted at the house of Anne Connells, a half breed Indian secured and carried away two free Negroes and an Indian besides setting fire to and wholly destroying all her houses, fodder stacks and movable property generally including two hundred dollars in bank bills. This Sir I have from the suffering woman herself and who is now on the point subject to interrogation by yourself the stolen Indian I am happy to say subsequently made his escape and is also with me.

On the 10th inst. I was informed a body of troops under the command of Capt. Willborne usually styled General came within two miles of my camp whether it was their intention to repair for the purpose of scouring it and make prisoners of all the Warriors, Capt. Brodner was the _____ of Capt Wellborne's intentions and also a request for me to meet him at Durants Stage Station on the edge of Cauley Swamp __ Fearful some depredations might be committed upon the Indians I repaired without lots of time to the place appointed and much to my chagrin and mortification found some six or eight of my warriors already prisoners.

I demanded of Capt. Wellborne his authority for their invading my camp. His reply was <u>the people</u>. I solemnly protested against the measure, that it was unnecessary and impolite, the faith of the Government was pledged to the warriors in Florida that those remaining behind should be wholly unmolested by the citizenry and placed under the protection of the Government that I *was the agent sent them by the Government and felt bound and was determined to protect the Indians. I was then given to understand the object of their march would be accomplished, notwithstanding my protest. I then asked Capt. Wellborne to appoint a committee to wait on me at the spring house at 3 Oclock P.M. when I would pledge myself to present all the warriors of my camp, to him they also objected and now still determined to raid the camp. Finding such to be their purpose I deemed it prudent to cooperate with them in order to prevent alarm and I save the Indians from being driven into the swamps, than good will to my unwelcome visitors. Capt. W. was willing to adhere to any course that I would suggest stratagem & deception, even my only wish to carry into effect the object in time to make a continuance of good faith on my part to the Indians----I therefore advised the immediate release of the warriors in custody and the counter march of the forces beyond the Calebee Swamp, then to remain until the arrival of a _____ from me. I had an understanding with Capt. Willborne that we should take a formal parting & when he should again make his appearance, I would positively insist upon his retiring without molesting the Indians that he might find assembled for the purpose of being mustered and every other day practiced. This I considered the only course of _____ my standing. At 2 Oclock the temporary chiefs reported their people ready for roll call when I dispatched a messenger to Capt. Wellborne who in a short time with four companies three of which were mustered into the service. Capt. Wellborne's, Capt. Harrods's, Capt. Young's and a Wm. Park, with a company of citizens from Rupert County surrounded my spring house , much to the amusement of the Indians, for instead of being alarmed, were delighted at what they deemed an unnecessary movement towards making them prisoners. I had stationed my interpreter near in order everything that transpired might be communicated to the Indians which being done, they appears perfectly satisfied with the course that I had pursued. I then appraised them their being made prisoners was not the act of the Government, on the contrary General Jesup would not continence such proceedings to remain perfectly quiet and everything would end satisfactory.-----Their reply was they looked to me for protection, that thus far it had been afforded and they know the Government would not desert them I reassured them all that General Jesup had promised their chiefs would be rigidly adhered to-. They appeared (and I have every reason to believe) were satisfied.*

I stated to Capt. Wellborne that in as much as the warriors now in bondage and taken away from their wives and children, protection should be afforded the latter, that I as also the Indians were apprehensive the soldiers would annoy them, he gave me positive assurance that they should not be molested. In order to satisfy Capt. Wellborne (who appeared more anxious to gain the applause of the disorganized soldiers than the public good) I called the role and found of two hundred & fifty three warriors fourteen absent, some of whom had been excused from attending muster in consequence of sickness and age etc. He was satisfied with the order of the camp or rather so expressed himself to me. A little after dark I heard the report of a musket in the direction of Thlobthloceo town (Jim Boy's) I stated to Capt W. it was unusual to hear a musket or rifle fired in the camps at that hour. I was apprehensive some mischief was being done by the troops, and begged a party might be dispatched to ascertain the cause. Five moments had elapsed after making their requisitions, when a second report of muskets heard in another direction. I then told Capt. W. he afforded me no protection, the warrior men upset telling me my tongue was forked, and for the first time I was holding bad talk. Capt. W. headed a party in person and set out in the direction of the firing, about 11 Oclock. He returned and informed me an old man was killed and a little girl wounded, that the marauders belonged to a Wm. Parks Company of Citizens of Rupert County Alaba. I demanded of Capt. W. the arrest of the whole of that company as it only comes to pursue in order to satisfy my warriors, that unless it was adopted a stigma would rest upon him and further, it would be the means of reestablishing me in the confidence. He agreed and said positively my wishes should be carried forthwith into effect, but such was not the case. On the following morning Wm. Park together with his denominated officers attempted to make an apology for the offense of their company. I told them the matter now rested with the Government nothing could be done by me but to pacify my aggrieved Indians, which was partially done by taking Wm. Parks and his associates before the Indians and pointing them out as the persons having authority over the men who committed the murder. I told the warriors, notice had already been taken of the offense and of their misfortunes, that an express had been sent to Fort Mitchell with all the facts connected with their sufferings that their men Wm. Parks and his associates now regretted the occurrences of the night and were willing to make any atonements for the losses sustained. The acting chief of Jim Boy's town (Hollis Hadjo) replied it was out of their power to bring life back he therefore would leave it to me to say what was best to be done.—I told them the old man was dead, died violently it was true, but life could not be restored we therefore must submit the reply was I was satisfied they were. I told them no, far from it, but we were obliged to submit in this case, but justice should be rendered. General Jesup would not suffer them to be imposed upon. Previous to this in company with Capt. Wellborne and Hollis Hadjo, I visited the house of the aged murdered man who proved to be Loch chi Yohola, about 90 years of age who had been excused owing to the infirmities of age _____ from attending muster at the Spring House found him lying in one corner shot in the breast and his head literally stove in with as I supposed butts of muskets.

With some difficulty I obtained permission for the son of Loch chi Yohola to leave the chain of sentinels. I afterwards found the little girl who had slightly wounded in the leg by a musket ball. She is the daughter of Loch a Finico of the Uffala town about fifteen years old. She stated the men wished to ravish her she refused and ran towards a thicket which was nearby when she was fired at. I am happy however to say she has entirely recovered. There are two warriors by the names of Catcher Finico belonging to the Uffala town the father of the girl is with me, the other is in Florida. Upon prosecuting my enquiries from them I learned the same men had in several instances accomplished their diabolical will upon the frightened women and in many cases deprived them by force of finger and ear rings and blankets, many of their women and whole families under a state of alarm ran to the camp where the major part of them are still and no doubt viewed as hostile. I have used every possible means to draw them out without success—the most prominent measure adopted was causing staffs with white muslin attached to be carried through the camps as a token of friendship. The question with the officers of the several companies what was to be done with the warriors now presented itself: nine of twelve were in favor of removing them to Tuskegee. I formally protested against it & proffered to leave the nation with my whole party rather than consent to a separation of my people. It was some time before they assented to my proposition as soon as informed of their _____ I repaired to Montgomery County and consulted the citizens residing in the vicinity of Wm. Higgs who readily acceded to my wishes and aided in the situation of an eligible situation for encamping. On my return I communicated with the Indians gave them the choice either of going to Tuskegee as prisoners and separating from their families or leave the nation with them.---there was no hesitation—they preferred the latter and in thirty six hours afterward with but four five horse teams, my party of upwards of 1900 strong was on the march. On the 22nd inst. I arrived at an encampment near Wm. Meigs without any murmuring or discontent except regrets for loss of property and suffering for the acts of guilty. The excitement of the citizens in the immediate vicinity of Pole Cat Springs Capt. Young's Company and a portion of Capt. Wellborne's against the Rupert County men was so great that so soon as it was ascertained my camp would be removed, deemed it prudent to leave at the earliest period, taking with them some eight or ten ponies stolen from the Indians.—of this fact I was informed by persons who met them on the road with the ponies in possession—indeed the conduct of this party was of the most outrageous and disgraceful kind ever persons in the public employ and the stores were wholly disregarded. One of the former was most violently beaten and otherwise maltreated and stores for the subsistence of Indians were taken by force.

As to the main inquiry...to wit—the probable loss sustained by the Indians and forced removal of my Indians, I answer, it is impossible to form a correct estimate within the time required, but can do so within a few days, as it will be necessary to call up the heads of families under the superintendence of their respective Chiefs—I am convinced their losses were heavy in ponies, cattle, corn, furniture and farming utensils etc.

Signed   Jno G Reynolds

1st Lt. U.S.M.C.

Within days of forcing Reynolds' group to head out of the area to Tuskegee, the militia surrounded

another encampment in charge of Marine Lt. Thomas T. Sloan. They forced all the Indians to gather

around Sloan's quarters and made them stay there overnight threatening them with being taken prisoner.

The militia members made several forays in the Indian encampments carrying off horses, and other

properties. Sloan was finally ordered by them to move the Indians out of the area. There were no wagons

to load all their belongings, so Sloan had the Indians store their goods in his headquarters area until they

could send wagons back for the goods. Unfortunately, once they left, the goods were plundered by the

undisciplined citizen militia.

Sloan reported,

Fort Morgan
Mobile Point
March 31st 1837

Sir

*In answer to your enquiries in relation to the outrages that have been committed on
the families of the Indian warriors serving in Florida, and the loss of property
incident thereto, I submit the following report.*

*In consequence of a disturbance that occurred at the plantation of Dr. Battle on the
Cowiga Creek, about the latter part of December last, thirty mile distant from the
camp under my control, (Echo Harjo's) I ordered the warriors forthwith to
surrender their arms and remove within a smaller compass, so that they might be
more immediately under my observation. This movement was made, not from a
belief that the depredations were committed by my Indians, (for I have no doubt it
was the remnant of the old hostile party that had never surrendered) but to appease
the citizens, and prevent any intercourse with my camp, some of whom had
previously been hostile; and sixty-three guns were deposited in my quarters.*

106

This order was promptly obeyed, and all of the old people of Echo Harjo's Indians, and a few of those that had surrendered, were encamped in less than half a mile square; the rest precipitately left the camp. They remained in this situation till the 5th of February, when I found my camp suddenly surrounded by an armed populace, headed by a Mr. Garnigan, and a party of Citizens from Georgia, a Mr. Park at the head of citizens from Russell county Alabama, and a Capt. Morris of Franklin County Georgia, that had recently been mustered into the service of the U. States. The Indians indiscriminately were immediately driven up around my quarters, I there guarded until twelve o'clock the next day, without provisions & in most instances a blanket to shelter them from the inclemency of the weather. I protested against their conduct as inhumane, uncalled for, and contrary to the solemn pledges of the Government, and that it would be more honorable and soldier-like to punish the aggressors, than harass a few unarmed friendly men, women, and children. After pillaging several of the Indian houses of property, and in one instance of <u>money</u>, they determined to remove the Indian men & <u>boys</u> to Tuskegee and place them within the stockade, under a strong guard, and permit the women & children to remain immediately around my quarters. The guns belonging to the Indians were also carried away by them and have not been returned. I have since understood they selected the best for their own private use. On the same evening my camp was again visited by two companies of citizens from Pike & Barbour Counties Ala headed by a Mr. Curry and Mr. Harrold - the latter company was that day mustered into service. After some conversation I succeeded in satisfying them, that no great danger was to be apprehended from a parcel of women and children, and after remaining until about midnight and plundering the houses of the Indians that had been abandoned, they left to join their associates in arms, about five miles distant, where they, that night, had encamped with the Indian men and boys. We had a respite from this ---- till the 20th of Febry when Park and his mob returned and after parading through the camp, took six men that had been frightened off on his previous visit; and, if the statement of some of his own men can be credited, stole two mules and a horse, and perhaps some ponies, & left the camp. On the 21st a Lt Ash, with a detachment from Capt Morris' Company, arrived at the camp and surrounded it, and after searching it thoroughly left for Tuskegee, without making any discoveries of a very <u>alarming</u> character. On the next evening I received a note from Capt George whose company was also in the U. States service & Lt Ash informing me that on the next morning they had determined to remove the women and children of my camp to Tuskegee. As I was that day making an issue of provision for five days, I begged them to defer it for four days, until they could consume their provisions, as no wagon were furnished for their transportation, it would be impossible for their transportation, it would be impossible for them to carry it, I requested to hear from them that night by express. No intelligence was received, and I was convinced the adhered to the determination, and on the morning of the 23rd ordered the Indians to prepare to remove to Tuskegee, & in half an hour the whole camp was on the march. In consequence of having no means of transportation, I directed them to deposit their effects in my quarters, & c, until wagons could be procured to remove them to Tuskegee; but in the mean time the *house was broken open and plundered of most articles of any value (I) we had proceeded alone within four mile of Tuskegee before we met the companies that were to <u>guard us</u>. They escorted us to Tuskegee, & encamped the women and children around the pickets under a guard, where they remained until they 7th? of March, when they were marched off by the same company to Montgomery, Alabama.*

The following is the description and value of the property that has been lost, as far as can be ascertained in so short a period.

145 Indian ponies (average value $30.00) $ 4350.00

60 Head of Cattle (average value $12.00)   720.00

200 hogs (average value $3.00)   600.00

100 Bushels of Corn (at pr. bus - $2.00)   200.00

100 Bee Hives (at pr. hive - $2.00)   200.00

Cooking & Farming utensils & Crockery ware 200.00

63 Guns (average $10.00)   630.00

Sacrifice in hurried sales of property   1200.00

Money stolen from Tallow war harjo   250.00

Total $ 8350.00

Very Respectfully
T. T. Sloan
Lt. & Mil. Agt. [9]

After the Indians left the area, Wellborne's men scoured the area for others and fought a brief engagement killing forty or more Indians. The two groups of Indians were moved and concentrated at Montgomery, and by March 8th, there were nearly four thousand of them.

General Jesup in Florida heard of this and protested the treatment of the families of his Indian allies and insisted that they be compensated for all the property that was stolen from them. He had to keep the Creek volunteers several months beyond the planned February release date which caused the local militias to try to force their families out at that time.

On March 20th, sixteen hundred of the refugees were loaded onto two steam boats and sent down river to Mobile Point. The remainder followed days later and there they remained in an encampment until July when the warrior volunteers under Jim Boy were returned from their service in Florida. Disease set in amongst the detainees at Mobile Point, and it was decided after a delegation of them inspected other areas for a more suitable camp, that they would be moved to Pass Christian, Mississippi, there to await transport by steam boat to their new lands. The death toll from disease while at Mobile Point and their removal to Pass Christian mounted to over two hundred and seventy, mostly from dysentery.

At Pass Christian, the officers in charge had a difficult time keeping whiskey drummers from selling liquor to the Indians. Lt Reynolds and Lt Sloan, accosted the peddlers and destroyed several barrels of whiskey. Local authorities arrested the two, charged them with starting a riot, but approved their actions in destroying the whiskey. They were fined one hundred dollars each for their actions.

The two officers corresponded with the Indian Commissioner some of the situations that they had to deal with:

Pass Christian, Miss.
31st July 1837

Capt.

In obedience to your call, I herewith furnish a statement of the deaths that have occurred in my Party since our arrival at Mobile Point, and at this place, the first death occurred on the 20th March, from that to 31st July, 177 deaths have taken place, 93 of which number died at the Point and 84 is since disembarking at this place. On 20th July 13 persons died and on the following day 12 being the greatest number on any one day.

The attending Physicians Report, I herewith enclose.

I am Sir
Very Respectfully
Your Obt. Servt.
Jno. G. Reynolds
1st Lt. U. S. Mil
& Disbg Agt Ind. Dept.

Capt. John Page
Superintendent Creek Emigrating
Pass Christian Miss

Pass Christian, Miss.
13 Sept. 1837

Sir,

I have the hour to report the arrival of sixty Creek volunteers from Tampa Bay; the officer in charge informed me, the remainder are on their way hither; so soon as they arrive, mustered out of service and paid off there will be nothing to detain us from moving. The sickness of New Orleans can easily be avoided with the aid of the civil authority, to prevent the Indians from straying, we can pass through, with but a few hours detention.

The mustering out officer and pay master will be here in a day or two. I hope your views as to an early movement will be given as soon as practicable.

I am Sir,
Your Obt. Servt.
Jno. G. Reynolds
1st Lieut. U. S. Mil.
& Disbg. Agt. Ind. Dept.

C. A. Harris Esqr.
Commr Indian Affairs
Washington City10

Reynolds corresponded with the Alabama Emigrating Company officials about their contract:

Indian Encampment
Pass Christian, Miss.
18th Sept 1837

Gentlemen,

The Contract entered into by the U. States with your Company, not embracing water conveyance for the Emigration of the Creeks, and it being the positive direction of Maj. Genl. Jesup, Comdg Army of the South, that this party be transported with every ease and convenience as well as comfort. I have to request in obedience to the wish of the Comdg. General; that the Company will provide by the date specified in my communication of the 16th inst. Steam Boats for their transportation, each Boat to accommodate and carry, not to exceed five hundred Indians. The land transportation, as defined in the contract, is such as will render the sick and infirm exceedingly uncomfortable, you are theretofore directed that instead of one Wagon for the number of persons and weight of baggage as expressed in the contract, to furnish two, the best of their kind.

As it is the wish of the Maj. Genl. Comdg. that every necessary article for the comfort of the party on the Route be furnished, I have to request you to inform me, the kind of provisions it is the intention of the Company to issue, agreeably to the Contract.

I am Gentlemen
Very respectfully
You Obt Servt
Jno. G. Reynolds
1st Lieut. U. S. M. C.
Disbg Agt. & C.

Messrs Wm. A. Campbell
& Wm J. Beatie
Agents and members
of the Alabama Emgtg. Company 11

Through the rest of the summer groups of the Creek volunteers arrived from Tampa Bay. It was not until October 29th that the first group set out from Pass Christian for the western lands. Lt Sloan was in charge of this group totaling sixteen hundred men women and children, all of whom were loaded onto nine steam boats. One of the boats, the *Monmouth* with six hundred and eleven Indians on board collided with another steam boat when the pilot of the *Monmouth* took a channel in the river meant for the opposing traffic. Over three hundred Indians drowned or were killed in the collision.

The late departure date of the Indians was due to the contractors objecting to having to provide land transportation for part of the journey. Reynolds had to consult with Washington to rectify the situation. These Indians had been forced from their earlier encampments by the militia groups and had been deprived of their own horses and means of transportation, resulting in the need for the extra wagons and teams to pull them.

The Seminoles

One of the first groups of Seminoles for removal originated at Fort Moultrie, South Carolina, where they had been imprisoned to prevent their escape as Chief Wild Cat had done from the Fort at St. Augustine. Lt Reynolds was put in charge of taking these Seminoles which included, Micanopy, Cahadjo, King Philip and Little Cloud. The party consisted of 116 warriors and 82 women and children, and Reynolds had a detachment of twenty-nine soldiers. They boarded the brig *Homer*, and landed in New Orleans on March 12, 1838. Five of the Indians died on the voyage. They were housed in barracks at Fort Pike to await others.

1837 Amy Navy Chronicles

The Indian prisoners who have for some time past been in confinement at Fort Moultrie, left Charleston on Friday, 16th inst., for New Orleans, on their way to the far west, in the brig Homer, Capt. Nabh. The Chiefs were embarked on Thursday morning. Lieut. Reynolds, of the U. S. Marines, will have them in charge.

NEW ORLEANS, March 14.—Lieut. Reynolds, of the Indian Department, and connected with the removal of the Creeks, who summered at Pass Christian this last season, arrived at this port on Monday evening, in the brig Homer, from Charleston, in charge of 215 Seminole Indians; among whom are Micanopy, King Philip, Cloud, and Coahajo, the principal chiefs. They are now stationed at the barracks below the city. Today Lieut. Reynolds goes to Fort Pike, for the purpose of removing the Indians over to this city, and as soon as the necessary arrangements can be made, they will be conveyed up to Arkansas. The party is in good health. — True American.

The steamboat Renown, Capt. McGuire, arrived at Little Rock May 26th, from New Orleans, with 455 Seminole Indians, under charge of Lieut. Reynolds, and passed up the same night. About 150 Spanish Indians, who have intermarried with the Seminoles, have also passed up. None of the Indians were permitted by the sentries to come ashore while the steamer stopped.

'From the Little Rock Gazette, July 25. SEMINOLE INDIANS.—Between 60 and 70 Seminole Indians came up on the s. b. Itasca, from New Orleans, on Saturday morning last, in charge of J Reynolds, U. S. Marines. They are part of Alligator's tribe, and that noted chief, with his family, are of the party. Take them as a body, they are as likely a party of Indian emigrants as we have seen, and we understand they are perfectly healthy." [12]

Reynolds then was dispatched to Tampa Bay, and from there, brought another group of Indians and Negroes on May 14th. By this time there were now 1,160 detainees awaiting passage to the west.

He took charge of the entire group, which was embarked onto steam boats on May 19th, the *Renown* was loaded with 453 Indians, and the South Alabama had 674 and Reynolds on board. A third of these were Negroes who had grown up among the Seminoles. The party reached Vicksburg, Mississippi on the 26th. By that time, 47 had died of disease, and five babies were born. The *Renown* reached Little Rock, Arkansas on May 26th but could not go more than 100 miles further due to the low water. The party included 90 Negroes that had been held back from the Creek volunteers the year before. They had been promised them as they had captured them, however, fraudulent claims made by slave traders held them in New Orleans.

James Watson supposedly purchased them from the Creeks for 14,000-15,000 dollars however General Gaines managed to hold up the sale. The Seminoles that had reached New Orleans by that time, claimed most of the Negroes as their property which had been stolen from them. When Reynolds left New Orleans he had managed to take most of the contested Negroes with him. Collins' partner Nathaniel Watson caught up with them at Vicksburg with an order from the Indian Affairs Commissioner for Reynolds to release the Negroes to Watson.

Micanopy and the Seminoles protested rightfully claiming this was a violation of the agreement made between them and General Jesup. Reynolds did not have troops enough to back him up so he appealed to the Arkansas governor, who declined to assist him. Even when he reached Fort Gibson, General Arbuckle refused to help him. Reynolds finally managed to return south and retrieve the ninety Negroes, and Watson filed suit in Congress for reimbursement.

Reynolds and his group of Indians were not able to get past Little Rock due to the low water so he had to have his Indians transferred to two smaller steamboats, the *Liverpool* and *Itasca* both of which towed two keep boats behind. On June 7th, King Philip died just fifty miles from Fort Gibson. The entourage stopped long enough to bury him in a casket. Reynolds had his guard members assemble and fire a salute over the grave in respect to the old chief.

Reynolds and his party reached their final destination at Fort Gibson with 1,069 of the 1,160 individuals that they had started with.

Reynolds made another trip from New Orleans on the *Itasca* with another 66 Indians including the chief Alligator and his family. They picked up another group of Seminole Negroes who had been delayed at Clarksville due to low water. They had to give up on river travel when they neared Fort Coffee, and Reynolds had to arrange wagons to carry them and their supplies the rest of the way, arriving at Fort Gibson on August 5th.

Chapter 6 Marines Who Served

When Colonel Commandant Archibald Henderson volunteered his Marines for service in the Indian wars, it was the first large scale mobilization of the Marines since the War of 1812. The Marines were pulled from the several Navy yards and from headquarters in Washington City. When they gathered they were organized into companies to serve in Alabama and Georgia. The organizational structure was as follows:

Colonel Archibald Henderson

Lt. Col. Samuel Miller

Brevet Lt.Col. Freeman

Captains Levi Twiggs Company **A**, John Harris Company **B**, P.G. Howle, Adj't and inspector E. J. Weed, Major and Qtr Master, William Dulany Company **D**, James McCawley, Brevet Captain Benjamin Macomber Company **C**,

1st Lieutenants H. N. Crabbe, Asst. Qtr. Master H.B. Tyler, George Lindsay, Acting Quartermaster. 2nd Battalion, Francis C. Hall Assistant Commissary, F.N. Armistead, George H. Territt 1st Lt. Company A, William. E. Stark, Alvin Edson, Commanding Company **F,** William Lang

2nd Lieutenants J.T. Sprague, Assistant Commissary, E. L. West, William L. Young, Josiah Watson, D.D Baker, Louis F. Whitney, Robert C. Caldwell,

James Gatchell Sergeant Major

John A. Kearney, Surgeon U. S. Navy

The Marines who served in Florida also included:

1st Lt John Ross (died of wounds received at the battle of Wahoo Swamp)

1st Lt. John Reynolds (distinguished service in Florida and later in the Civil War)

1st Lt. Waldron of the West Indies Squadron

When General Jesup was ordered to Florida, along with his own troops, he brought Henderson with the Marines and Indian forces. The Marines at that time consisted of:

18 OFFICERS 303 ENLISTED

The following year after Henderson took a large portion of the Marines north with him, he left behind under Lt. Col. Miller, then Captain William Dulaney who served under Jesup:

4 OFFICERS 170 ENLISTED

This did not include Marines that served off of the ships of the West Indies Squadron. They mostly served in the mosquito fleet in and around Southern Florida. One notable compliment of Marines from the Squadron of the *USS Concord* which served time both around Tampa Bay and Fort Brooke, also manned Fort Foster twenty-five miles north of Tampa Bay. They fought a few skirmishes with the Seminoles at Fort Foster. These are the Marines of the *USS Concord* as listed by Navy Lt. Mervine Mix in his journal in the special collections of the University of South Florida:

Sgt. Jos. J. Wright

Corpl. Jno Robinson

" Wm. Thornton

Private Jas. Byrnes

" Francis Bowsfield

" Robert Cole

" Orlando Gatfield

" Jno. Harris

" Jas. Hayes

" Adam Holt

" Jno. Humphreys

" Jno. Kolby

"   Michael Kirmine

"   Peter McMannus

"   Barney McCaffrey

    Jno. Madden

"   Wm. Pace

"   Benj. Richards

"   Chas. Rugg

"   Wm. Snyder

"   Patrick Shea

"   Jno. Shoemaker

"   Jno. Wilson

As in most wars, the majority of deaths were not from wounds in battle but from disease, especially in a climate such as Florida which most of these men from the north were unaccustomed to. Here is a list of the Marine casualties of war in Florida.

Marines of the Regiment who died

Name	Rank	Company	Place of Death	Date	Cause
Thomas P. Peterson	Drummer	B	Hatchelustee Swamp	Jan. 27, 1837	Killed in action
Joel Wright	Private	B	Hatchelustee Swamp	Jan. 27, 1837	Killed in action
Andrew Ross	1st Lt.		Fort Heileman	Dec. 11, 1836	Wounded at Wahoo
William Tait	O. Sgt.	E	Post Sannibar River	Dec. 5, 1837	Disease
Henry Marks	Sergeant	A	Fort Brooke	Nov. 9, 1836	Disease
George King	Sergeant	D	on ship from Tampa	Aug. 3, 1837	Disease
Charles Pike	Corporal	D	Tampa Bay	Apr. 14, 1838	Disease
Matthew McKinley	Corporal	E	Tampa Bay	Apr. __, 1838	Disease
Daniel Brown	Private	D	Chattahoochee River	Oct. 13, 1836	Disease
John Shillingsford	Private	E	Fort Brooke	Dec. 7, 1836	Disease
John Reardon	Private	C	Fort Brooke	Mar. 14, 1837	Disease
William W. Vancleaf	Private	D	Tampa Bay	Feb. 21, 1837	Disease

Alexander Burke	Private	E	near Fort Armstrong	Jan. 20, 1837	Disease
James O'Neil	Private	E	Fort Brooke	Mar. 1, 1837	Disease
William Steel	Private	B	Black Creek	Aug. 11, 1837	Disease
John H. Durant	Private	D	Fort Brooke	June 29, 1837	Disease
John Sweany	Private	E	Tampa Bay	Apr. 27, 1837	Disease
Michael Sullivan	Private	A	Fort Brooke	July, 15, 1837	Disease
J.M. Waalfin	Private	C	Mullet Key E.F.	Aug. 22, 1837	Disease
Issac Elburn	Private	D	Fort Monroe	Oct. 1, 1837	Disease
William J. Henry	Private	D	Fort Dulaney E.F.	Nov. 17, 1837	Disease
John Jackson	Private	D	Fort Dulaney E.F.	Nov. 22, 1837	Disease
Richard Trask	Private	E	Tampa Bay	Apr. 2, 1838	Disease
John A. Perley	Private	E	Fort Denaud E.F.	Feb.3, 1838	Disease
Thomas Fling	Private	E	Columbus, Ga.	Sept. 11, 1836	Disease

Marines of the Regiment Wounded in the Florida War

Name	Rank	Date	Location	Wound
Daniel Cunningham	Sergeant	Jan. 27, 1837	Hatchelustee Swamp	Both Shoulders
Leonard Stevens	Sergeant	Jan. 27, 1837	Hatchelustee Swamp	In the thigh
Peter Foley	Private	Jan. 27, 1837	Hatchelustee Swamp	In the arm
John Sullivan	Private	Jan. 27, 1837	Hatchelustee Swamp	On the lip
Thomas Irwin	Private	Unknown	Fort Armstrong	Accidental shooting

Marines of the West Indies Squadron who died in the Florida War

Thomas T. Starke	Corporal	Dec. __, 1839	Steamer Poinsett E.F.	Disease
David Cannon	Corporal	Sept, 4, 1841	Indian Key	Disease
Frederick Dunn	Fifer	Nov. 4, 1841	Indian Key	Disease
Henry Elisha	Private	Aug. 21, 1841	Indian Key	Disease
Joseph H. Root	Private	Sept. 24, 1841	Indian Key	Disease
James V. Sawyer	Private	Oct. 6, 1841	Indian Key	Drowned
Joseph Smith	Private	Oct. 6, 1841	Indian Key	Drowned

James J. Ayer	Private	Nov. 11, 1841	Indian Key	Disease
Thomas Ennis	Private	Nov. 25, 1841	Indian Key	Disease
Robert Gray	Private	Nov. 20, 1841	Indian Key	Disease
John Nicolson	Private	Dec. 23, 1841	Indian Key	Disease
Andrew Kelly	Private	Dec. 26, 1841	Indian Key	Disease
Stephen Schoolcraft	Private	Dec. 9, 1841	Indian Key	Disease
Jacob Schultz	Private	Dec. 6, 1841	Indian Key	Disease
William Williams	Private	Dec. 16, 1841	Indian Key	Disease
Rufus Griffin	Private	Jan. 16, 1842	Fort Dallas	Disease
Lorenzo D. Pierpont	Corporal	Jan. 20, 1842	Fort Dallas	Disease
Jeremiah Kingsbury	Private	Mar. 14, 1842	Fort Dallas	Disease
Thomas Walsh	Private	July 18, 1842	Schooner *Flirt* at sea	Disease

Those listed as Indian Key were in the hospital that the Navy built there. Several others were shipped north as they were in very serious condition and unlikely to survive without better facilities and treatment than what was available in Florida.

Marines of the West Indies Squadron wounded in the Florida War

William Smith   Acting Corpl Jan. 6, 1841   Wounded in a skirmish with Indians

Uniforms and Equipment

The basic uniforms of the Marines during the 1836-1842 period changed. The dress uniform was green coat, with buff trim. Trousers were grey in cold weather, and white for summer wear. The 'tar bucket' style of shako with gold eagle plate and yellow pom-pom topped it off. The winter fatigue uniform which was worn in the field was of gray wool trimmed in yellow piping and the summer fatigue uniform was of the same high-waist style made of white cotton duck material. The proper fatigue hat was the flat style leather forage cap resembling the 'mechanic's' style civilian cap and not the high-standing model 1833 forage cap of the army as represented in modern paintings of the period. The flat style forage cap as shown in the picture of the author in a previous chapter is the correct style. This is confirmed by the drawing of the sailors and Marines landing at Quallah Battoo in 1832 by a crewman who witnessed the landing. Also an advertisement in a Baltimore newspaper for the capture of two deserters describes them as being dressed in their gray fatigue uniforms and flat topped leather fatigue cap. Shoes were standard issue same as the style of the army.

Accouterments were white belts with oval breast plate and rectangular belt buckle and black leather cartridge box and bayonet with scabbard. The standard wooden 'cheese box' style canteen was used, along with the standard haversack for food, and backpack for uniform and personal items.

Late in the War, the Marines changed uniforms to a style that resembled the artillerists of the army as pictured in the painting "Sailors and Marines Crossing the Everglades" in a previous chapter.

The weapons carried by the Marines were the standard model 1816 musket in .69 caliber, with bayonet. It is recorded that the Marines did try out the Colt revolving rifle, however after five men were injured due to malfunctions from being loaded for a number of days, they returned to the musket. A limited number of Hall's 1833 breech loading muskets were used, but they tended to foul up too quickly.

The standard model 1836 flintlock pistol in .54 caliber was the most common side arm. There were several different manufacturers of these and in different calibers. It is possible that some of the officers may have purchased the new Colt revolver.

Swords if they were carried would have been the standard nco and officer swords of the period.

Appendix 1 FORTS MANNED BY MARINES

During the Second Seminole War, almost 200 forts, cantonments, and camps were built. Many of these were used as supply depots for the troops operating in the field. Most were built two days march apart. Many of the smaller ones were nothing more than enclosures for overnight protection constructed of logs laid out, three high.

These are some of the forts manned by Marines at one time or another during the seven year conflict.

Fort Brooke at the mouth of the Hillsborough River on Tampa Bay near today's Platt and Franklin Streets.

Fort Foster twenty four miles north of Fort Brooke (Tampa) on the on the Fort King Road that ran between Fort Brooke and Fort King (Ocala). It was located at the site of the previous Fort Alabama alongside the Hillsborough River, situated by the bridge. A replica was built near there in the Hillsborough River State Park.

Fort Clinch at the mouth of the Withlacoochee River on the north bank halfway near Yankeetown.

Fort Dade on the southwest bank of the Withlacoochee River north of Fort Foster just south of the county line of today. Burned by Seminoles in 1838, later rebuilt downriver just north of the present-day county line on the west side of today's US 301 / FL 35

Fort Fraser near Bartow, on the east bank of the Peace River near Peace Creek

Fort Van Swearingen six miles northeast of Lake Okeechobee on Van Swearingen Creek.

Fort Lauderdale a full fort with a two-story square blockhouse was originally near the forks of the New River between present-day SW 8th and 9th Aves. Abandoned and then burned by the Seminoles. Re-established in 1839 on a new site east at the Tarpon Bend. It was later abandoned.

Fort Dallas was named for Commodore Dallas established by the U.S. Navy, at the mouth of the north-side of the Miami River. This was not a log stockade as other forts, but a collection of tents and small buildings. The Army took over in February to March 1838, moving the post to the opposite side of the river. The Army referred to it as Fort Bankhead. The Navy took it over again in 1842.

Fort Kemble along the Miami River built and manned by Marines to protect the wood cutting parties of the naval squadron.

Fort Dulaney at Punta Rassa at the mouth of the Caloosahatchee River.

Fort Denaud E.F. (East Florida) (at present day Denaud)in the 'Charlotte Glades' midway between Lake Okeechobee and present day Fort Meyers, two miles from the Caloosahatchee River. It was built by Captain B. L. E. Bonneville one of a series of forts linked together for the operations in south Florida. It consisted of several tents with a blockhouse in the center on land owned by Pierre Denaud. This also served as a supply depot for the troops in the Lake Okeechobee area.

Fort Armstrong at the site of Dade's Massacre along the Fort King Road near Bushnell.

Fort Center on the south bank of Fish-eating (Thiathlopopkahatchee) Creek. This was a blockhouse to store supplies.

Appendix 2: List of Ships of the Florida Squadron June 1838-August 1842

The list of vessels in the Florida Squadron from June 1838 to August 1842 commanded by Lieutenant John McLaughlin consisted of the *Wave, Panther*, and revenue cutters *Campbell* and *Ostego* with 160 men until November1839.

From November 1839-June 1841, it consisted of the *Flirt, Wave, Ostego*, and barges *Mayo* and *Harney* along with two companies of Marines totaling 41 men.

From June 1841 to August 1842, it was made p of the *Flirt, Wave, Ostego, Phoenix, Jefferson, Madison, Van Buren*, and the two barges with 130 Marines totaling 622 men which included 68 officers. Along with the ships and barges, 140 canoes were used.

The main supply depot for the squadron was on Indian Key which was garrisoned by Marines as well as Fort Dallas.

List of Ships of the Florida Squadron June 1838-August 1842

Date	Vessel	Lieutenants Commanding
1838-39	Schooner Wave	John T. McLaughlin
1840-41	Schooner Wave	John Rogers
1841-42	Schooner Wave	Acting Lt. John C. Henry
1838-39	Sloop Panther	Acting Lt. E.T. Shubrick
1839-41	Schooner Ostego	Acting Lt. E.T. Shubrick
1839-41	Schooner Ostego	Acting Lt. James S. Biddle (Revenue Service)

1838-39	Schooner Campbell	Lt. N. C. Coste (Revenue Service)
1839-41	Schooner Flirt	John T. McLaughlin
1839-40	Barges Mayo, Harney	Acting Lt. Montgomery Lewis
1840-41	Barges Mayo, Harney	Acting Lt. C.R.P. Rodgers
1841-42	Schooner Phoenix	Acting Lt. C.R.P. Rodgers
1841-42	Brig Jefferson	John Rodgers
1841-42	Schooner Madison	William L. Herndon, Acting Lt. W.S. Drayton
1841-42	Schooner Van Buren	John B. Marchand

The following steamers also saw duty with the squadron, Steamer Cincinnati, Steamer James Adams, Steamer Poinsett under the command of Captain Mayo

List of Ships of the West Indies Squadron 1836-1838

These ships saw duty around the coast of Florida, however they also patrolled the Gulf as Far as Mexico, and throughout the Caribbean.

U.S.S. Constellation

U.S.S. Vandalia

U.S.S. Motto

U.S.S. St. Louis

U.S.S. Concord

Sloop Cumberland

Brigantine Calvin

Notes

Chapter 2

1. Hunted Like A Wolf by Milton Meltzer

Chapter 3

1. 1836 Diary of General Jesup Beinecke Special Collection Library, Yale University

2. Archibald Henderson Papers U.S. Marine Archives

3. 1836 Army Navy Chronicles

4. Archibald Henderson Papers U.S. Marine Archives

5. 1836 Army Navy Chronicles

6. 1836 Army Navy Chronicles

7. Samuel Miller Papers U. S. Marine Archives

Chapter 4

1. 1836 Army Navy Chronicles

2. 1836 Army Navy Chronicles

3. Mervine Mix Journal University of South Florida Library

4. Flames Over the Lighthouse by Harry Caygill Leatherneck Magazine March 1955

5. Mervine Mix Journal University of South Florida Library

6. Amidst a Storm of Bullets Diary of Lt. Henry Prince in Florida 1836-1841

7. Miserable Pride of a Soldier 1836-1839 The Letters and Journals of Col. William S. Foster in the Second Seminole War

8. Miserable Pride of a Soldier 1836-1839 The Letters and Journals of Col. William S. Foster in the Second Seminole War

9. Samuel Miller Papers U. S. Marine Archives

10. Samuel Miller Papers U. S. Marine Archives

11. Samuel Miller Papers U. S. Marine Archives

12. 1836 Army Navy Chronicles

13. Mervine Mix Journal University of South Florida Library

14. Mervine Mix Journal University of South Florida Library

15. Archibald Henderson Papers U.S. Marine Archives

16. Amos Eaton Papers Miami University Library

17. Amos Eaton Papers Miami University Library

18. 1838 Army Navy Chronicles

19. 1838 General Jesup Diary University of Florida Library

20. A Canoe Expedition Into The Everglades in 1842 by George Henry Preble digital collections Tequesta files

21. A Canoe Expedition Into The Everglades in 1842 by George Henry Preble digital collections Tequesta files

22. Notes on the Passage Across the Everglades The News-St Augustine January 8, 1841

Chapter 5

1. Indian Removal by Grant Foreman

2. Indian Removal by Grant Foreman

3. Indian Removal by Grant Foreman

4. Sprague Letters

5. Sprague Letters

6. Sprague Letters

7. Reynolds Letters in the Ethan Allen Hitchcock collection, Beinecke Collection Library, Yale University

8. Reynolds's Letters in the Ethan Allen Hitchcock collection, Beinecke Collection Library, Yale University

9. Sloan's Letters in the Ethan Allen Hitchcock collection, Beinecke Collection Library, Yale University

10. Indian Removal by Grant Foreman

11. Indian Removal by Grant Foreman

12. 1837 Army Navy Chronicles

Bibliography

Buker, George, *Swamp Sailors in the Second Seminole War*   University Press of Florida 1975

Caygill, Harry, *Flames over the Lighthouse*   Leatherneck Magazine March 1955

Dixon, Anthony, Black Seminole Involvement and Leadership during the Second Seminole War 1835-1842 https://scholarworks.iu.edu/dspace/bitstream/handle/2022/7603/umi-indiana-1694.pdf?sequence=1

Foreman, Grant *Indian Removal: The Emigration of the Five Civilized Tribes of Indians,* University of Oklahoma Press January 1975

Henderson, Archibald Commandant, USMC *Papers of Archibald Henderson* in the United States Marine Corps Archives

Jesup, General Thomas Sidney *1836 Diary of General Thomas Sidney Jesup of the Creek Campaign* in the Beinecke Special Collections Library of Yale University

Jesup, General Thomas Sidney *1837 Diary of General Thomas Sidney Jesup* in the Florida State Archives

Jesup, General Thomas Sidney *1838 Order Book of General Thomas Sidney Jesup,* in the special collections library of the University of Florida

Kimball, Christopher, *Seminole and Creek War Chronology,* Lexington, Ky., April 2013

Mahon, John *History of the Second Seminole War 1835-1842,* University of Florida Press1991

Meltzer, Milton *Hunted like a Wolf* the *story of the Seminole War*, Pineapple Press 1972

Metcalf, C.H, *When Our Commandant Took the Field.* Marine Corps Gazette February 1936

Miller, Samuel, *the Samuel Miller Papers* in the United States Marine Corps Archives

U.S. Marines in the Second Creek and Second Seminole Wars by David Ekardt

Preble, George Henry Rear Admiral USN, *A Canoe Expedition into the Everglades in 1842*

http://digitalcollections.fiu.edu/tequesta/files/1945/45_1_03.pdf

Prince, Henry Lt., *Amidst a Storm of Bullets Diary of Lt. Henry Prince in Florida 1836-1841,* University of Tampa Press 2006 Edited by Frank Laumer

Sprague, John *The Origins, Progress and Conclusion of the Seminole War*, University of Tampa Press 2000

Other Collections

Army Navy Chronicles 1836

Army Navy Chronicles 1837

Army Navy Chronicles 1838

Army Navy Chronicles 1839

Army Navy Chronicles 1840

Army Navy Chronicles 1841

Army Navy Chronicles 1842

"Notes on the Passage across the Everglades" THE NEWS - St. Augustine: January 8, 1841

http://digitalcollections.fiu.edu/tequesta/files/1960/60_1_06.pdf

Websites

http://www.northamericanforts.com/East/fl.html

http://www.keyshistory.org/IK-massacre-1.html Indian Key massacre

http://freepages.genealogy.rootsweb.ancestry.com/~texlance/emigrants/index.htm Creek Emigrants to the Western Creek Nation

http://indians.passchristian.net/index.htm

http://scholar.library.miami.edu/Eaton/   Amos Beebe Eaton Papers Miami University

http://freepages.genealogy.rootsweb.ancestry.com/~texlance/emigrants/index.htm   Letters of

Reynolds and Sloan

U.S. Marines in the Second Creek and Second Seminole Wars by David Ekardt

Printed in the USA
CPSIA information can be obtained
at www.ICGtesting.com
LVHW011931311023
762689LV00012B/470